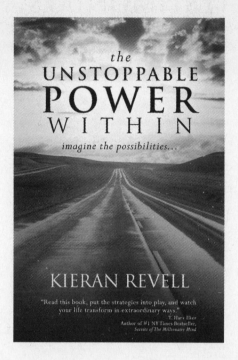

Rationale for Cover

THE WONDROUS JOURNEY OF YOUR LIFE

The wet road denotes that into your life, some rain must inevitably fall. It's the rain which makes your life worthwhile, exciting and exhilarating because overcoming challenges is what makes you come alive.

The rain ultimately delivers the cleansing of your doubts, worries and fears.

Although the road is not always smooth, you continue with absolute faith, hope, courage and optimism.

As your life progresses, the clouds give way to the amazing sunshine. Your world becomes brighter.

Optimism and passion grow with your beliefs as you journey onward.

You discover powerful faith in yourself and the road you are travelling while embracing a whole new perspective of your future.

TESTIMONIALS

In this wonderful and ground-breaking work, Kieran has opened the door wide to the possibility of success and prosperity for each and every one of us. There can no longer be any excuse for failure.

Read this book, put the strategies into play, and watch your life transform in extraordinary ways.

T. HARV EKER
Author of #1 *New York Times* bestseller,
Secrets of the Millionaire Mind

Practical, impactful, and inspirational. Each one of its many chapters could transform your life!

DR. JOHN F. DEMARTINI
Bestselling author of *The Breakthrough Experience*

Kieran Revell has really surpassed the mark with his book, *The Unstoppable Power Within*. A powerful book offering easy to follow steps to creating your optimum life. This book is a must-read for anyone who seriously wants to discover their unstoppable power within.

BOB PROCTOR
Bestselling author of *You Were Born Rich*

This wonderful book is a guide and an inspiration to each person trying to overcome difficulties and make the best of his life.

BRIAN TRACY
Bestselling author, professional speaker, and success coach

In his new and inspiring work, *The Unstoppable Power Within*, Kieran offers readers a unique opportunity to bring success and prosperity into their lives. Rich in wisdom and knowledge, each extraordinary chapter of this groundbreaking book provides priceless advice on living the most incredible life possible.

You cannot afford to procrastinate any longer as your life blithely passes by. Don't wait until tomorrow to begin the practice of empowerment. Make up your mind to be the best you can be and begin your exciting journey to an extraordinary future today with this book.

DR. JOE RUBINO
CEO, CenterForPersonalReinvention.com
Creator, TheSelfEsteemBook.com
Bestselling author of 12 books available
worldwide in 23 languages

In *The Unstoppable Power Within*, the quotes alone deliver so much power that within them are the keys to massive personal transformation.

KRISTEN HOWE
www.lawofattractionkey.com

This book, *The Unstoppable Power Within* is a must read for anyone wanting to get to the next level in their life. There are too many resources out in the marketplace that really miss the mark and are very confusing .... BUT this isn't one of them. This book is filled with common sense advice and information. If you want the right tools to get to your dreams and aspirations then buy this book.

JUSTIN HERALD
International Entrepreneur of the Year 2006
Author of 8 international bestselling books

I believe this wonderful work will become one of the great classics. Its timeless wisdom and resounding messages give people a clear path to success. *The Unstoppable Power Within* will transform lives—it is powerful, simple, and moving.

TERRY HAWKINS
and founder of People in Progress and Terry Hawkins Enterprises
Professional speaker and educator
Author of *Why Wait to Be Great? It's Either Now or Too Late!* and
Stickman Rules (children's series)

The Unstoppable Power Within provides the reader with a true and lasting blueprint for success. It is without doubt a must-read for the inspired individual or business owner searching for that one key to change to a wonderful and empowered life. Shine a bright light on the path ahead and build the life you've only ever dreamed of.

There is no magic wand for success, but through the strategies outlined in Kieran's wonderful work you will begin to empower your life and move to a point of absolute prosperity. The wisdom Kieran has put into print is pure gold.

Apply the principles and you will soon understand what it means to be incredibly successful and abundant. Stop procrastinating and apply the principles today. If you do nothing else this year, buy this wonderfully empowering book and put the principles into action. Take action today and transform your life forever in extraordinary ways.

JAMES MALINCHAK
Featured on ABC's hit show, *Secret Millionaire*
Founder, www.bigmoneyspeaker.com

In *The Unstoppable Power Within*, Kieran tapped into timeless knowledge and wisdom and created a powerful guide to a more successful life. It's a step-by-step guide you will refer to time and time again.

JIM DONOVAN
Author of *This is Your Life, Not a Dress Rehearsal*

Kieran Revell's book *The Unstoppable Power Within* is a brilliant, step-by-step guide to harnessing your potential and breaking through the limitations that have held you back.

I recommend you buy this book, but more importantly I recommend you apply the wisdom in this book to live the life of your dreams.

TOM McCARTHY
Peak performance specialist
Professional speaker/trainer, author,
consultant, executive coach

Kieran has tapped into a tremendous well of knowledge to write a very potent and powerful guide to creating a successful and abundant life. The chapters present an easy to follow guide for those who wish to establish themselves as truly successful beyond their wildest dreams.

CHRIS WIDENER
Author of *The Art of Influence* and *The Leadership Rules*
www.ChrisWidener.com

All of us have dreams and ambitions. Some of us even know we have a vehicle to get from where we are to where we want to be. Very few of us know that we can steer our own vehicle directly into our destiny.

Kieran has provided a road map and driving lessons that can make the difference for you. You are one step away, and that next step may lie between the covers of this book.

JIM STOVALL
President and co-founder of Narrative Television Network
An International Humanitarian of the Year
Motivational speaker and author of *The Ultimate Gift*

Kieran Revell has written a fantastic book, titled *The Unstoppable Power Within*. What is most amazing is how the author skillfully weaves words into a simple yet elegant road map for all those who aspire to find success on the pathway of life. I love the stories used as examples in this book. This is definitely a *must*-read. Thanks, Kieran, for sharing such life-affirming information with us.

JOHN HARRICHARAN
Award-winning author of the bestseller, *When You Can Walk on Water, Take the Boat* and other books

If you want to truly fast-track your success, this book shows you how. Read it all in one sitting or take each step and work through it day by day. Either way, you'll get impressive results when you follow Kieran's advice.

STEPHANIE FRANK
Bestselling author
President, Success IQ University
www.SuccessIQU.com

Kieran is an author who focuses on the energy of words. Words can empower or disempower, create clarity or confusion.

In this book you will take notice of the words you choose to energize and the result that will give you is nothing short of transformational.

MIKE HANDCOCK
Chairman and founder of Rock Your Life
International Bestselling author

I have read probably close to a hundred inspirational books and I consider *The Unstoppable Power Within* as one of the most perceptive and transformational books on success and empowerment in the market today.

This book is incredibly inspiring and the principles are simple to put into practice. It provides a systematic pathway to success with an easy to follow route map.

I believe that this book will inspire readers to take focused action to unleash their inner genius to empower them to live life to their fullest potential.

DR. YKK (YEW KAM KEONG, PH.D.)
Chief Mind Unzipper and Innovation Consultant
Mindbloom Consulting

Brilliant—a wealth of information. Kieran Revell's *The Unstoppable Power Within* is the most important book you will read this year.

Applying the principles in this book will transform your life. Buy this, borrow this, or steal this book, but whatever you do, read it now and start living the life you've always dreamed of!

Akash Karia
Professional speaker and public speaking coach
Hong Kong
www.CommunicationSkillsTips.com

Kieran writes with true passion and depth and provides a wealth of information on the subject of success with suitable digests from many of the top thinkers, entrepreneurs, and mindset specialists on this area.

One definitely gets the impression that this author is positively willing you to succeed in every way to live a purposeful life.

Kath Roberts
Life and business coach

If you want to read just one book this year, *The Unstoppable Power Within* is the one I'd recommend. I have always believed that we as human beings are powerful beyond measure, but most of us need guidance to awaken the power within; Kieran is such a guide.

In his book, he takes you by the hand and shows you how to go from learning the basics to making things happen.

Kieran has a magnificent gift to guide and help others understand what is needed to realize their potential; from inspiration to manifestation of one's goals and desires, he covers it all.

If you feel you are ready to go from good to fabulous in your life—this is it!

Tamara Baruhovich, Life coach
http://Transforming-My-Life.com

I can't think of anyone who wouldn't benefit from reading this book. Kieran's manuscript is amazing. It is so well written that you can't help but be drawn in.

I challenge you to read Kieran's book. You will be glad you did.

LANCE HOOD
Peak potential and business strategy coach

Kieran Revell's approach to life is fantastic. His knowledge, passion, and programs deliver the tools, resources, and strategies necessary for everyone to accelerate their success.

If you are looking to maximize your potential and realize your dreams, look no further than right here.

If you want to stay where you are in your life, *don't* call Kieran.

WARREN A HENNINGSEN
C.E.O., My Absolute Success Pty. Ltd.
International bestselling author
Speaker/teacher/writer
Relationship builder/personal success mentor
Mindset trainer/personal awareness expert

the
UNSTOPPABLE
POWER
WITHIN

Tammy Fitzgerald—Editor

Eileen Rockwell—Cover Design

Sound Wisdom
P.O. Box 310
Shippensburg, PA 17257-0310

For more information on foreign distribution, call 717-530-2122.
Reach us on the Internet: www.soundwisdom.com.

ISBN 13 TP: 978-0-7684-0681-8
ISBN 13 Ebook: 978-0-7684-0682-5

For Worldwide Distribution, Printed in the U.S.A.
2 3 4 5 6 7 8 / 18 17 16 15

the
UNSTOPPABLE
POWER
W I T H I N

imagine the possibilities…

KIERAN REVELL

Life is not a dress rehearsal; it's the main production. The satisfaction you achieve and accolades you receive will depend upon your drive, passion, vision, and self-belief and your ability to capitalize on opportunities as they arise. Do this and it will be the performance of a lifetime.
—KIERAN REVELL, 1989

DEDICATION

This book is dedicated with heartfelt love and affection to:

My beautiful wife Suzanne and my incredible son Kayle, who through their endless love and support continue to bring boundless sunshine into every aspect of my universe.

My mum and dad who always guided me, loved me, and taught me to act with integrity, passion, and optimism in spite of the circumstances faced. Thank you! May you forever rest in peace.

My darling brother Paul. You're loved and remembered every day for your zest, passion, and wicked sense of humor.

ACKNOWLEDGMENTS

The only ticket you need to ride the Success Express
to abundance will be stamped with self-confidence,
drive, determination, passion, gratitude, and vision. Then
you'll know clearly that all things are possible.

I am eternally grateful to the love and support from my beautiful, thoughtful, and caring wife Suzanne. She remains my source of unfathomable inspiration every moment of every day—without exception. She has an inquiring mind and unmatched strength of character which nurtures my courage and determination.

It's impossible to imagine a life without the unending love and encouragement of the most beautiful person in the world. She remains my rock.

A huge loving thanks to my wonderfully gregarious and extremely creative son Kayle. He warms my heart and makes me smile every day. His great mind remains unconstrained as he goes from strength to strength with his awesome ideas and designs. His talent never ceases to amaze me.

They remain the two most precious and important anchors in my life and continue to put the richness and color into every millisecond of my magnificent world.

A special thanks to Dr. YKK (Kam K. Yew, Ph.D., www.mindbloom. net), the world's leading authority on Creative Innovation. He has been an immense support and source of great information on this amazing journey. Himself a bestselling author, YKK continues to be a well of knowledge and a great sounding board for ideas and information.

I also offer a heartfelt thanks to the wonderful team at Sound Wisdom Publishers for their unwavering faith in me, both as an author and a speaker/ consultant. I especially thank David Wildasin as the face of the company and his consistent belief that together, we could deliver something fresh and new to a global audience.

I also thank John Martin and Tammy Fitzgerald for the exceptional editing of the book and of course, Eileen Rockwell for the amazing cover design: It literally took my breath away.

When there is a cohesive team working seamlessly towards a common goal, the end result is a product of which we can all be immensely proud. The endless support from these extraordinary team members has been overwhelming.

Thank you to the amazing photographer Ian Mora for the great photograph on the back cover.

Every day offers me the opportunity to grow and learn through meeting focused, passionate, and driven people with countless moments to add value and color to my life.

Thank you to my many loyal clients, supporters, and readers who are also my friends. Your passion for life and boundless enthusiasm continue to enrich my world.

I wish you the success you deserve as you continue on your incredible journeys to some amazing destinations. Never give up and always hold yourself in high regard.

Imagine the possibilities...

Failure should only ever represent a momentary lapse. It's simply a bump in the road to incredible abundance.

CONTENTS

FOREWORD

Without doubt, *The Unstoppable Power Within* is a definitive work on creating the kind of life you desire, no matter who you are or what your current circumstances might be.

The idea of manifesting success and abundance in life is not a new concept. However, in this very thought provoking work, for the first time this topic has been taken to a unique and innovative level of understanding. Kieran has added a new and exciting dimension to the very real notion of igniting prosperity in your life in a well-structured, step-by-step program.

Far too often, individuals labor under the misapprehension that what they currently have (or do not have) in their lives is all they will ever enjoy. This misnomer can be quite debilitating because it sets the individual up for inevitable failure through destroying creativity, drive, passion, and vision to such an extent that those same people fail to recognize and therefore grasp opportunities to excel in one or more areas of their lives. As a sad consequence, they never realize their full potential.

The Unstoppable Power Within is a tremendously groundbreaking work which establishes a very solid framework for untapped success and prosperity through the adoption of a specific program of dreaming, creating, planning, acting, and realizing. Written in upbeat and easy to understand terms, this book highlights a complete success and prosperity strategy.

This wonderfully engaging book removes the mystique from an often misunderstood topic and outlines a very tangible and easy to follow step-by-step program. If you are committed to capitalizing on the many great opportunities which present themselves in your life every day, then consider this work a must-read. Follow the chapters and apply the dynamic principles and you will set yourself up for inevitable success and prosperity.

After reading this book and applying the principles, there is absolutely no excuse for failure. As Kieran rightly points out, success is a right and not a privilege.

I recommend this powerful work to anyone wanting to get from where they are now to a point of absolute prosperity. Apply the principles and watch your life change in extraordinary ways.

Loral Langemeier
Bestselling author of *The Millionaire Maker*
Coach, author, professional speaker, and mentor
www.liveoutloud.com

INTRODUCTION

Don't look up for the sunshine in your life—look within.
The warmth and magic of success begins with the notion
that you are the most wonderful person in the world and
the source of immeasurable beauty and happiness.

Success and abundance are within reach, with clear and unimpeded access to the knowledge, wisdom, and tools to develop a wonderful and impacting future. Others have cut a path through the darkness for us to follow. Each of us therefore needs only to open our minds and hearts, embrace the material, and set sail for our own unique destiny.

Congratulations on your decision to step into the sunlight and embrace this wonderful chance to realize a new and inspired life. It's the first confident stride on your tremendous journey of discovery—of yourself, your wonderful life, and the abundance which surrounds you every day.

This first volume opens the door on the possibility of success and prosperity in your life. In a comprehensive, step-by-step process it shows you just how to harness your inner potential, alleviate your fears, and instigate some fundamental changes in your life and the lives of those around you.

Each chapter is a complete step on the journey to personal and professional fulfilment. As you finish one, begin to put the principles into practice with passion and purpose and watch as your life begins to change in extraordinary ways.

Enact that effective plan today and begin your inspired journey. When you appreciate the everyday experiences that bring color and abundance into your life and you have true and unbridled drive, enthusiasm, persistence, and gratitude, there'll be no impediment to all you can achieve. Success will rise up to meet you.

> The quickest and most direct route to success is found in one's self-belief. Drive and persistence to embrace abundance and a refusal to accept setbacks are simply fuelled by determination.

Having studied the lives of many successful people; spoken to motivational leaders; and spent thousands of hours of study and application, trial and error, questions and answers, learning lessons and overcoming obstacles, I'm convinced that success and abundance are within reach of us all. We need only believe in the journey we're taking and begin the process.

I have no doubt of the limitless power of the human spirit. Through our connection with this wonderfully abundant and generous Universe, we each possess an unfathomable depth of untapped wealth and talent, which shines brightly within. In every corner of our being it drives our words, thoughts, feelings, emotions, and actions. It's the core of our very existence.

In this first volume of Kieran Revell's groundbreaking work on personal and professional development, we are introduced to the immeasurable power of the human spirit—an amazingly vibrant life source. It provides all we need to be successful, caring, loving, gracious, thoughtful, wise, thankful, compassionate, resourceful, dedicated, and successful human beings. When we can put our spotlight on the hub of this incredible power and harness its purity, it allows us to focus our attention on just what is fundamental in our lives.

In spite of what might impact us, we each possess the inherent power to harness greatness in one or more aspects of life. Our journeys can be heavily influenced by differing backgrounds and ambitions and the impact of our innate belief patterns. We can be impacted by the way we interact and how other people treat us. All these aspects conspire to shape our words and actions in response to everyday problems.

> Problems are like potholes in the road—often unavoidable. However, having stepped in one, you can choose to step out and move on or decide to stay where you are and wallow in self-pity. The future will unfold regardless.

No matter who we are, we (generally) do *our* best to be *the* best. Whether a carpenter, plumber, speaker, waiter, mechanical engineer, office manager, mentor, pilot, teacher, police officer, football coach, doctor, personal assistant, athlete, delivery driver, paramedic, painter, nurse, cleaner, taxi driver, actor, fire officer, shop assistant, public servant, sanitary worker or undertaker, we seek to connect with that euphoric state associated with success and achievement in all aspects of our everyday enterprises.

> Out of seemingly abject failure will come monumental success when you find and nurture the strength and courage to continue on your path.

Success and prosperity in life are certainly within reach of us all. This is an undeniable fact based upon my own life journey and the many outstanding examples set by exceptional people around the world who strive selflessly to make a difference in the lives of others.

Given the vast instances of triumph over adversity we read in the press every day and the stories of incredible successes throughout recorded history, I have no doubt of the enlightening power of humanity and those who strive to embrace it.

> Success is possible in the lives of each of us, no matter our individual circumstances. We must first believe we deserve it then plan, prepare, and fully expect it without doubt.

There are those who constantly think of new and innovative ideas but don't actually convert them into reality (they remain simply dreams), while others begin and successfully complete project after project (converting dreams into reality). Even within our own circles, many start but fail to finish projects while others seem to sign off on them one after another. There are those who try very hard but can't seem to finish in first place, when others constantly stand triumphantly at the podium for whatever activity they undertake.

It can happen in the confines of the home; in the office, the supermarket, the gym, or on the sporting field; perhaps in the street, the car, your garden, or at the home of friends. None of us knows where or when problems will strike or in what manner or intensity. It depends on various factors—the influences you have and the quality of your life, the actions (and inactions) you take, the company you keep, the environment in which you live and the degree of interaction with others, your state of mind, belief in your journey and how you think you figure in the big scheme of things, your understanding of your innate abilities and the degree of self-belief and feelings of self-worth you cultivate. The world is a big place, true enough, but it need not be daunting.

Over the years I've heard much of the same rhetoric: "I don't have the time to read," or, "How can anyone know what's good for me?" There is, of course, my favorite: "What can a stranger tell me that I don't already know?" I understand the fear, uncertainty, and frustration these people are experiencing through similar thoughts I had some years ago. I began reading the plentiful information in the marketplace on the important topic of personal and professional development. I began to freely and confidently decide what was important in my life and take the steps to embrace it.

You too will understand just how your own thoughts, words, and actions impact directly on your world in the same way as the many outside influences you encounter each day.

If you view your life in terms of limitations and expectations and believe that you are only capable of reaching a certain standard, then I guarantee you will forever regret not having tried to achieve everything that's possible in a world where there are no limitations or boundaries to success and abundance.

Remain focused, confident, and determined to rise above adversity and embrace the success which will present itself in your life in many forms and through various opportunities every day.

The information presented in this book is a solid blueprint for success and prosperity. Enjoy the inspiring journey ahead and continue to nurture and support the genius within! You deserve it.

Imagine the possibilities...

Chapter 1

DARE TO DREAM

Once you learn to turn up the voice of the dreamer inside
and turn down the babble from the doubter, you will be on
your way to greater success and abundance in your life.

The wonderfully enigmatic Walt Disney put it so succinctly when he said, "If you can dream it, you can do it!" The dream of a better existence is the initial expression of your desire to step away from a sometimes scant and mundane existence and begin the process of living an extraordinary life. Dreaming is not simply something you do during your sleep, only to forget the images when you wake. This process is just the beginning. It creates the very building blocks of a profoundly exciting and empowering existence.

There is a defining difference between the individual who is a dreamer and the one who dreams of a more colorful, exciting, and prosperous existence. It's the context of those dreams—how they're brought to life and where they actually lead—that effectively shines the light on their priceless power and value.

The design for a successful future commences when you have absolute faith in yourself and begin to formulate your plans for a better life. Your desire for improvement across all aspects of your world will drive you to take action to create something incredible with your vision, courage, and determination, based on those powerful dreams. That inbuilt yearning for the very best you can do across all aspects of your life is the beginning of the process.

By fueling that burning desire, you begin to build on your dreams. This is the beginning of the journey to creating the ideal life—doing the very best you can. Your drive and determination set in motion your strategic plan to begin that process of creation and evolution. This in itself is a priceless gift and worthy of hard work and diligence.

Wealth will come from living your dreams when you understand the importance of putting your plan in place and fueling it with drive, persistence and gratitude. When you are doing what truly drives you and fills your heart with warmth and color, you will be living a life of success and abundance. Your entire attitude will change and even more opportunities will begin to manifest in your life.

Michelangelo di Lodovico Buonarroti Simoni (the gifted Italian Renaissance sculptor, painter, architect and poet) was a brilliant thinker and creator. He's credited with the immortal words, *"The greatest danger for most of us lies not in setting our aim too high, but in setting our aim too low and achieving our mark."*

The difference between success and failure is not just one's ability to dream but the courage to follow them and take the steps necessary to embrace success.

History reminds us time and time again of the tremendous successes of those who have gone before and forged a path with the courage and determination to create profound abundance from their dreams through to the creation, development, and ensuing achievement of incredible and inspirational goals. This action will very often lead to a better and more abundant life, greater wealth and prosperity, happiness and good health, and countless others which fuel the passion and desire to move forward with purpose.

Many of the visionaries throughout times past have found the courage and determination to develop unparalleled business and personal enterprises from a willingness to dream, plan, and act—often in the face of almost overwhelming opposition.

There are many who continue that brilliant journey today through the countless thousands of exceptionally successful projects which continue to bring unprecedented levels of wealth and freedom to those with the courage to pursue them. These driven individuals who exhibit the vision, determination, and functional plan of action give life and color to their wonderful dreams of a better future.

> The only thing which will get in the way of success and abundance is your own narrow view of life and your inability to believe in yourself and your dreams.

The great Napoleon Hill is the brilliant father of positive thinking and the author of such international bestselling books as *Think and Grow Rich, Master Key to Riches, Law of Success in 16 Lessons,* and *Unlimited Success: 52 Steps to Personal and Financial Reward and Success Through a Positive Mental Attitude.* He espoused the very profound and evocative words, "Whatever the mind can conceive and believe, it can achieve.

> You can't hear if you don't listen, feel if you don't reach out, or see if you don't open your mind and your heart.

It became a tenet by which he lived his amazing life. It should feature prominently on the mast head of the journey of every person serious about attracting and maintaining success and abundance in every aspect of life.

Success, however, certainly doesn't happen by accident; it occurs through design. You must have the correct tools, implement the right strategies, and fire your passion with maximum focus and dedication to prevent anything negative from standing in your way and obstructing your view.

Success is really so close at hand. You yearn for great things, and that desire turns into dreams. They eventually become reality with the right plan in place and the appropriate action.

Everything you have in and desire from life is the product of your imagination which is constantly influenced by many competing aspects. If you give power to the negative elements which come into your life, they can impact adversely on your future. They will take root and eventually cover your life like a blanket. You must constantly believe you have power over anything which can influence your imagination. It is squarely within you to create your ideal world.

You wouldn't jump from an aircraft without a parachute (some people would never do it, no matter what!). Likewise, you should not jump into your future without that special parachute—your open mind (and a clear plan of action). From that comes the ability to move forward with enthusiasm and a concerted effort.

If your dreams don't aim for the stars, you have the chance of only reaching as far as your outstretched hand.

Believe that great things are possible in your world and you're on your way. Feel good about yourself with no exceptions. Create the *success vibration* and release yourself from negative thoughts and emotions which are not in sync with your desires. Believe in yourself and your plan, your creativity and ideas, and you'll be well on your way to realizing great things in your future.

Decide now to be exceptionally successful and abundant; start thinking like a winner and champion; dream and focus in color and with great clarity. It has the power to drive your future to an incredibly abundant place.

Don't constantly blame other people and circumstances for the obstacles in your life. Take ownership and create your own reality by positive and results-driven dreams and goals and the appropriate action.

Finding success and abundance in your world requires effort, struggle, and very often a great deal of sacrifice. It takes courage to step from your comfort zone, like the tight-rope walker who decides to cross that ravine (even with a safety net, it appears fraught with danger). In spite of the opposition, the performer steps out with the courage and determination he/she knows is required to complete the task. Having long dreamed of this day and in spite of the innate and almost overwhelming nerves, the gutsy and courageous performer can taste success.

The only vision in the mind and heart of the performer is the point at the end—the goal on which he/she focuses absolute attention through an exhilarating journey undertaken with a resolve borne of the determination to accept nothing less than absolute success.

> If you can dream it, you can envisage it, you can think it, you can believe it, you can do it, and you can be it. Your life will be all you want it to be. Have faith in yourself and your ability.

Wallace D. Wattles, an extremely free and creative thinker, wrote many inspired pieces on overcoming mental barriers and how creation is, in fact, the real key to attracting wealth.

In his groundbreaking work *The Science of Getting Rich*, Mr. Wattles wrote, "It is a natural law that like causes always produce like effects; and, therefore, any man or woman who learns to do things in this certain way will infallibly get rich."[1]

Having a dream is certainly not daydreaming, though it can be part of the visualization process. Learn to focus on your goals and know beyond question you will achieve everything you strive for, in spite of any problems or opposition you'll surely face.

> Greatness does not occur by accident. Your clear vision, determination, hard work, and solid plan of action work in harmony to constantly raise the bar and help you achieve and maintain a level of personal magnificence.

Rise every morning and focus on the prize ahead. Know exactly what you want—see, feel, taste, and experience it in that very moment. Believe it's in your hands *now*—part of your reality in this instant, today, as a core component of your psyche. You deserve it. Be gracious and grateful for all you have and everything you wish to have in your life.

Make your dream fit your desire and perspective and be crystal clear in your vision. For instance, it's perhaps unrealistic at best to set your sights on being the leader of your country, the CEO of the biggest corporation in the world, or an Olympic gold medalist if you don't have the current skills, experience, drive, and determination to realize that lofty objective. Your goal must also be plausible, and if it's truly your dream, make it possible through effort and action. Develop the plan to make it come to fruition.

Choices must be based solidly on what you truly want from your life plan, your ability, the extent to which you're prepared to push yourself, and just how determined you are to capitalize on everything required to grasp it.

Your dreams support your ticket to ride the success train on your individual expedition, which you map through your visions of a better life and determination to achieve the very best existence possible. Paint your own colorful picture and build on it as you see your future unfolding.

A dream is the very beginning of that blueprint of success. It lays the mandatory foundations. If you can't dream of an optimistic and fulfilled future and clearly see positive and empowering outcomes, how can you possibly enact a plan to support it and set about achieving it?

To ensure you're on the right track to incredible success, never ask the question, "Why?" Always ask, "Why not?"

Persistence is the key to unlocking dreams, giving a firm direction in which to project your energy and action. It lays the very foundation of success and abundance and allows you to see your future in all its glory.

Dreams provide the vision of a greater future. Your plan of action indicates your belief that your incredible journey has begun, fueled with determination, focus, commitment, and attitude. This begins the progression to eventual abundance. The dream sets the mood; you begin to develop your picture of an incredible future.

Once you commence your magnificent system of creation, have the patience, courage, and persistence to step outside of your comfort zone whenever necessary and grasp all opportunities as they arise. They will, so be ready.

> An idea comes to you for a reason. Don't disregard it. Instead, write it down and store it. When the time is right, use it to formulate an incredible plan for the future.

Brilliant ideas about your life and your plan will come to you, seemingly out of the blue. We're surrounded by them every second of the day, yet we often fail to recognize or appreciate their significance.

There will be things which come into your life at any time but which you're perhaps unable to immediately adopt for any number of plausible reasons. Keep them safe in your journal. I firmly believe ideas (notions and offers) come to all of us for a purpose, as do problems and challenges. They have the capacity to open doors. I've learned never to disregard anything.

Any time an idea comes to you (or an offer is made), record it in your journal and date it. From good ideas come great plans and even greater successes.

> Always ensure your dreams have a true purpose. They must create a pathway to something better and more outstanding than you have now. Give them color and direction. Give them life. Give them heart.

In spite of the opposition you may face from others (and indeed your own insecurities), always move forward with your plans according to your own faith, passion, and vision. Empower your dreams to take you to places you would once never have conceived of going to nor had the courage to strive for.

Constantly update your journal and make the time to return to those shelved ideas and notions. Give them the attention and regard they deserve. Bring them into the bright light of day. They come to you for a reason and could just offer great new and inspired directions. Your journal will also be a wealth of support during difficult and trying times.

Use your journal/diary as a repository of dreams, great ideas, thoughts, and notions. Constantly refer to it to keep the momentum going and remind yourself of the reasons why you're on this particular journey.

Allow yourself the freedom to create the ideal life through your wonderful dreams. Take the journey often and enjoy every second of your mental creation as you begin the process of bringing them into the world of reality.

Build on your dreams with life and power. Never allow doubt, fear, or indecision to divert you from your chosen path. When others try to tell you how impossible your journey is, remind yourself of your innate power to achieve. Your dreams are the foundations of that awesome journey.

You can't underestimate the power and value of your dreams and ideas or trade them for anything less than you deserve. Your life is far more precious than that. *Respect it. Respect yourself. Embrace life.*

NOTE

1. Wallace D. Wattles, *The Science of Getting Rich* (Chichester, United Kingdom: Capstone, 2010), 11.

When you have a dream, a clear vision, and persistence,
time and patience become your best friends

LESSONS LEARNED

1. In spite of opposition, hold on to your dreams.

2. Your burning desire will assist in your drive to create your ideal life.

3. Be persistent in every positive thing you do.

4. Make your dreams clear and vivid.

5. The bigger you make your dreams, the bigger will be the reality you create.

6. Have the courage to step out of your comfort zone.

7. Allow your dreams to fuel your powerful plan of action.

8. Be persistent. There's a natural progression to where you want to go.

9. Include your dreams, visions, plans, ideas, and wishes in your diary/ journal.

10. Follow your dreams and don't allow others to steal or destroy them.

11. Don't allow doubt or fear to divert you from your goals.

12. Never underestimate the power and value of your dreams/ideas.

13. From good ideas come great plans and even greater successes.

14. Respect yourself. Respect your dreams. Respect your life.

Chapter 2

THE ESSENCE OF SELF-BELIEF

Change your belief patterns and you change your reality. That's
a truism that has the capacity to impact incredibly on your life.

No matter what you wish to achieve, you must believe in your ability and
support it with every fiber of your being. Make up your mind to be wealthy
and abundant, famous, philanthropic or a global charitable force and use
your ferocious state of mind as your driving force. If you have those negative blocks in your mind, you need to break them down systematically by
believing with every positive and focused thought you have that your ideal
life is coming together.

Every day we have options—small and large—which directly influence
the path we're traveling. We possess the power to instigate positive changes
through those impacting choices and the effects they have on our dreams,
goals, and desires. We must stay true to who we are and have faith.

You may wish to start a new business or perhaps a second or subsequent
as an additional stream of income—"ASI" (see Chapter 13). To do that you
might need to convince your bank manager to provide start-up capital or others to invest in your idea and then the customers to support your business
interests and provide the consistent funds necessary to assist your venture to
grow and develop.

Determination and drive are the enemies of fear and failure.

The fundamental difference between incredible success and *that other place* is as finite as a razor's edge. It's as simple as that—no ifs and no buts. It's a matter of choice. It's a sound and supported state of mind developed from the clarity of dreams, thoughts, words, and actions, fueled by determination and a relentless belief in the power of "the self."

When concentrating on your life and the direction in which you're traveling, there really are only three days which are of concern in the short term. The first two have the ability and capacity to impact adversely on the third if you lose your focus and allow your dreams to falter in the face of adversity.

Once you bring real and concentrated persistence to everything you undertake, failure becomes only a temporary postponement of success.

The first is *yesterday*, and we can do nothing about that. It has long since passed into history and is now a closed book in which reside our errors, worries, faults, misgivings, fears, challenges, shortcomings, and mishaps. It is also a repository for our past thoughts, words, visions, emotions, actions, and achievements—our smiles, successes, loves, and embraces. In spite of how it might have affected us as we passed through, it will not be within our control again.

We do, however, take from the past our experiences—the dreams and wishes for a bright and more prosperous future. We should not have regrets about yesterday but learn lessons and optimistically hold tightly to the dream of a time that is even better, more profitable, and more successful than we envision.

The second is *tomorrow*—a time of beckoning, a period of incredible optimism and endless possibilities, promises, and rewards. It is an era of infinite potential which has twenty-four hours—one thousand four hundred and forty minutes or eighty-six thousand four hundred seconds.

We know without question the sun will rise tomorrow. We may not always see it, but that incredibly powerful, bright, and life-giving globe will nevertheless travel along its extraordinary trajectory to its eventual setting. Tomorrow remains unborn, yet we hold great expectations for it. We impact on it through our wishes, thoughts, words, emotions, and actions but remain unable to do anything to hasten its arrival. It also has the potential to cause great consternation as we worry (unnecessarily) about what it might or might not bring.

> Learn to live in the moment—in the here and now. Understand that the most important things in your life are occurring in this instant. Do that and you free yourself up to build on the future.

The one important time in our lives is *today*—where we live and work in the moment. Each day holds the promise of wonder and fulfilment in a time when we can put into play our plans for a more incredible future. It's where we capitalize on everything positive which comes into our individual and collective consciousness. It represents the most crucial instant in our lives.

If we are to be truly successful, we must learn to accept the instant in which we're currently residing and allow it to occupy every corner of our being, for it's in this time we have the ability and capacity to create and subsequently build on our dreams and visions. In this state of pure love for and faith in ourselves, we find the courage and strength to strive for the magnificent things we know we are capable of achieving.

It's in this wonderful place where we apply our energy, effort, determination, and unerring belief to the positive action we take. This will certainly move us from where we are to where we want to be.

> Release yourself from your burdens and open the windows of opportunity in your life. Prepare to make room for greater success and abundance to flood into your world.

Don't add to the burdens of the day by embracing the emotional and psychological baggage of a combined force of yesterday and tomorrow. It's a pointless and ultimately destructive exercise. Take from them what you need to move forward but leave them where they belong and concentrate on the peaks and troughs of the moment. Adapt and evolve. Learn the necessary lessons and apply them to your thoughts and actions.

Focus all your positive energy on creating a spectacular future without any extraneous factors weighing you down. Learn to clear your mind and focus on your dreams. Always leave the troubles of the day in the realm where they were developed. Think of them in terms of a glass of water held in your hand. The initial weight is unimportant. However, the longer you hold on, the heavier it will become. If you hold your negativity for long enough, you will eventually succumb to the weight and likely surrender.

> Don't look back with anger or regret; always move forward with optimism and enthusiasm.

Your troubles might start out small, but if you continue to hold them inside they will become onerous and unbearable. It makes sense to leave them where they originate so you won't carry an unnecessary load on your shoulders. By doing this, you free yourself up to find functional solutions, and as a consequence your health and wellbeing won't suffer from the deleterious effects of unnecessary burdens.

If the weight of your troubles becomes too much, seek the assistance of a medically trained professional who can assist you to move forward through the threatening darkness.

Today is the day to believe unequivocally that you can attract wonderful things into your life when you understand the steps necessary to initiate positive change. These are tried and true measures, and with discipline and application they can work for you, provided you have a plan of action, strong self-belief, and dogged determination to succeed.

You can make incredible, life-altering changes simply by believing in yourself and your ability.

Throughout our lives we can and do have business and/or personal problems (often simultaneously) irrespective of who we are, where we live, and how much money and/or prestige we may (or may not) have. They are facts of life and can profoundly affect many areas of existence.

We frequently consider the problems which beset us to be all-consuming and overpowering, believing we can't and won't find a way out of the crushing maze. The problems often hang like a storm cloud above our life, affecting every waking (and sleeping) moment. They appear to magically compound themselves, and the light at the end of the tunnel seems to continually diminish.

In spite of what might be impacting our lives, there can be no doubt that right now is the ideal time to continue (or commence) a committed program for accumulating wealth, accelerating success, and striving to be the person we truly want to be (and know beyond question we're capable of becoming).

Problems which present themselves in our daily lives are simply guide posts toward a better path to achieve our destiny.

The world is brimming with more incredible, positive energy than ever before to help you achieve your goals. There are far more teachers, mentors, and drivers who have the wisdom, experience, and accumulated knowledge to assist you to achieve everything you know you are capable of bringing to fruition. You must first learn (without regret) to let go of some of those embedded beliefs which are holding you back. To reach your full, true potential, accept that change is inevitable and healthy.

Foster an unfailing belief in yourself and your ability; see your future in all its color and splendor and know beyond question that you are an incredible person who is on the right track and destined for greatness. Find the courage to step from your comfort zone into the brilliant sunlight of opportunity. Demonstrate your eagerness to accept success and abundance into your life. Make the right choices today and open that door.

> I am an abundantly successful person because I know I am. I allow nothing to divert me from my journey to incredible prosperity.

A solid and unswerving belief in ourselves and all we do is one of the greatest and most powerful tools we possess in our quest to be the best and most successful we can. It defines the very essence of who we are and what we as individuals (and groups) stand for. It remains an incredibly powerful component of life which pushes us to perform at our very best. For instance, if you enter a race, go for a job interview, undertake a home improvement task, or play a professional sport, you would never entertain the thought that you can't come out on top or that you would lose. To do that would be totally self-defeating and serve no positive purpose whatsoever.

Beliefs underpin every aspect of our daily lives as we continually formulate a series of patterns based upon our many experiences and our related reactions (a consequence of their impact upon our feelings and emotions).

There's so much which would not have been invented, created, developed, written, composed, erected, recorded, floated, collected, driven, spoken, or embraced if those who had the vision to move forward with purpose and passion did not have a total and all-encompassing belief in their own skills, drive, and vision.

Success and abundance—your destiny—are decided by the power you hold inside and your drive, focus, and self-belief. A very important step for progress is to learn to let go of the negatives of the past and actively choose success—deciding to be wealthy and successful in all aspects of your world. Put your life on a new and exciting track toward unrestrained abundance.

Everything we see, hear, feel, taste, touch, and think can and does impact us—favorably and adversely—at every turn. From an early age, our minds and hearts are like sponges as we soak up everything we experience. This is often done involuntarily as we subconsciously take in every aspect of our interaction with the world around us.

When you make the decision to inspire and empower your life, there's a specific path necessary to get from where you are now to where you wish to be. It is possible and probable if you believe in what you're doing and you have the courage, drive, vision, and determination to succeed.

If you desire enrichment in the more altruistic and meaningful areas of your life—such as love, respect, assistance, warmth, praise, security, compassion, generosity, trust, and truth—then you must behave in a manner which will compel others to freely offer these things to you. You must become a conduit for goodness and enrichment.

> Every failure you face and subsequently overcome brings you ever closer to your goal of greater success and abundance.

These more personal and introspective gifts must also be earned. When your words and actions induce these feelings of harmony and balance within yourself and positive responses from others, you'll know your life is on an inspired road to prosperity.

A vital part of this learning process involves dealing with those who are charged with the responsibility of building our character through the impact of their leadership, love, guidance, support, and encouragement. We must trust they have our best interests at heart. However, when we discover that an individual might not be working positively and in support of our highest values, we should seek professional assistance to right any abrogation of that responsibility.

From the cradle to the grave we continue to learn, whether intentionally or otherwise. Very often what we discover (or what bombards us on a daily basis) is at odds with our positive growth and development. Belief patterns are formed in our critical early years of development; reinforcement continues throughout our lives. It's those early belief patterns which assist in the formulation of our dreams, visions, and goals and the associated drive and power to succeed in spite of the many obstacles faced. We all have the power of achievement; we need only realize our potential and tap into it.

> Success is linked to your destiny. When it becomes part of your dream of a better life, fueled by persistence and self-belief, it will be an integral part of your existence.

Belief patterns have specific emotional tags attached to them, sometimes fueled by prejudice (born of ignorance and fear). They are largely inherent and build up from our early years as we continue to learn. They reside deep within us and are embedded in the subconscious. Therefore the impact they have on the way we live our lives is almost unavoidable. Those who pass them to us have learned from others, and so the unbroken chain continues unless we take control. Often we do not understand why we believe what we do; it's simply the result of the many influences in our lives.

> The only power more intense than a faith in God is an unshakable belief in yourself and your ability. Without that, you have a huge void in your existence which cannot be filled.

Often this outcome is unintentional. Those who seek to give us a strong and empowered future unwittingly give us their fears, foibles, and intolerances, systematically formed throughout their own lives. As a result, we develop patterns which are out of balance with our intrinsically positive feelings and therefore exert unnecessary pressure on our lives. Whether the influence of others is positive or negative, it nonetheless affects the way we see the world and consequently react to the various stimuli we face every day. This in turn will greatly impact the degree to which we find and enjoy any level of success.

When we have inherent negative and self-defeating beliefs, we can be overwhelmed by a cloud of crushing pessimistic pressure that has developed over time and therefore has the capacity to keep us shackled. Far too often we remain unaware of the effect this has on our lives and any impacting results are not viewed as unusual. They become a normal part of our existence.

From failure comes success, because in those trials you learn what not to do in order to be prosperous.

If we resign ourselves to the belief that all we have right here and now is all that will ever fill our lives, we've surrendered our futures to the devastating bleakness of negativity. We've bowed to those dark forces which compete with our positive thoughts and emotions in the hope of bringing us down.

Release the greatness you harbor deep within yourself and begin the life-changing journey toward incredible success today. It is possible and very achievable for all of us. Success beckons; you need only open your eyes and your heart and believe in yourself.

If you are truly committed to a more fulfilled life where you are literally overflowing with fresh and positive beliefs and your day is filled with creativity and success, you need to replace those negative principles which are holding you back and preventing you from moving forward to greater prosperity.

Make no mistake, while you harbor those self-limiting patterns your growth and development will be stilted and you will never find the courage or drive to rise to those incredible heights you know you are capable of achieving.

There are specific actions you can take to free yourself of the chains of past debilitating beliefs and establish more positive and uplifting patterns to add value, color, life, and depth to your world. It won't occur overnight, but you can still establish them as influential aspects of your existence through consistent application and ongoing attention. You will soon be on the road to recovery.

A positive attitude will change your life. You need only the climbing equipment of a solid plan of action, passion, determination, persistence, and gratitude to see you stand on the pinnacle and rejoice.

The following steps will assist you on your journey of reestablishment. *Make up your mind* that change is necessary if you are to have a more empowered life. Take control and identify those beliefs which are holding you back.

Look at your life and see those recurring patterns which your thoughts and actions have followed. Identify those critical areas where you've made poor choices due to the influence of your beliefs. Understand the difference between balanced and positive influences as opposed to those which detract from the quality of your desire for a magnificent life. *Have a clear understanding of your goals* and begin to establish new beliefs. They should be more in line with your desire for positive thinking, life improvements, and an empowered journey. Write them down and use them in the form of affirmations which you recite every day as you visualize and systematically recognize the positive and powerful impact they are having on your life. You can also pin them up throughout the home and office in strategic places and constantly refer to them, drinking in their value.

Dismantle the previous negative beliefs and begin replacing them with new positive thoughts. It will be a slow but worthwhile process and should be done at your own pace so you don't become dejected. One by one, begin the process of change through understanding the hold negative thoughts have on your life and the impact they have on your emotions, and embrace the change.

You can greatly assist this process through:

- Setting new and empowered goals in the process of repetition. It leads to ongoing reinforcement.

- Creatively visualizing the new behavior and associated feelings of power, success, and elation.

- Record your new and evolving beliefs, ideas, and visions in your journal and refer to them whenever you feel the need.

You reinforce the new values through repetition at any time of the day, particularly when old belief patterns begin to surface. This generally occurs in times of stress when you revert to the safety net of the old ways. Remind yourself why you've made the changes and how the positive impact is complimenting your life. The old will begin to dissolve once you establish a solid platform for the new patterns to emerge and continue with ongoing positive reinforcement.

The changes will be recognizable when you begin to see life from a new and exciting perspective through fresh and empowered eyes. You will also reap the benefits of improved positive thinking. *Once new patterns are established*, break the emotional bond to the old and create positive emotional ties to the new. Do it through affirmations, visualization, and meditation. Understand the value of the new processes in your life; decide that the old no longer have a place in your world. Embrace the reasons for the new and how they are impacting positively on your life. Now embed them in your subconscious mind.

Finally, give the new belief patterns a firm platform of existence in your life by empowering them. Align yourself with the new beliefs and embrace them for the wonderful impact they are having on you. Acknowledge the critical link they have to your existence. You are now in a position to fully embrace and sanction them.

> I am never afraid of what my life holds because I know I have the power, courage, determination, and love to overcome any obstacle and the passion, persistence, and belief to achieve monumental success.

Believe in yourself like never before. Allow nothing to stand in your way as you forge a path ahead to a brand new horizon. Once you have the strength of your convictions, others will also believe in you and your journey.

Now is the time to soar with the eagles at great heights and cease the wasted time spent fighting over scraps. There's no future in living a mundane existence. Empower yourself today and enrich your life with the very life blood of existence. Lose the fear and make the conscious decision to move ahead at incredible speed to a new and inspired future with fresh, powerful, and innovative belief patterns.

You have everything you need at your fingertips. Be courageous and step out of the shadows. No more excuses—induce the change and live an incredible life from here on.

> When we open our minds and hearts and ask for
> what we truly want, remain focused and certain of
> the ideal life we wish to live, and fully embrace it, the
> universe has an uncanny knack of giving it to us.

LESSONS LEARNED

1. One of the greatest tools we possess is our self-belief.

2. Everyday options (and subsequent choices) determine the road we're traveling.

3. There are only three days we need to worry about:
    - Yesterday: already passed into history and we can do nothing about it
    - Tomorrow: a time of endless possibilities, promises, and rewards
    - Today: the one important time in our lives

4. The difference between success and "that other place" is as finite as a razor's edge.

5. Throughout our lives we can and do have business/personal problems.

6. Difficulties need not be all-consuming and/or overpowering.

7. Believe with every fiber of your being in your ability to achieve.

8. Today there is more positive energy than ever to help you achieve your goals.

9. Belief patterns are critical to growth and development.

10. Foster an unfailing belief in yourself and your ability.

11. Release the greatness we all harbor and begin the life-changing journey to success.

12. Victory beckons; you need only open your eyes and your heart and believe.

13. Make the right choices today and open the door.

14. Choices have emotional tags attached.

15. Belief patterns are established throughout our lives.

16. What we believe, can exert unnecessary pressure on our individual and collective worlds.

17. Your destiny is decided by the power you hold inside.

18. Negative, self-defeating beliefs will keep you shackled.

19. Consistent attention to belief patterns empowers your life with depth and color.

20. Reestablishing positive belief patterns involves a five step process:
    - Make up your mind that change is necessary.
    - Have a clear understanding of your goals and begin to establish new beliefs.
    - Dismantle the previous negative beliefs and replace them with your new positive thoughts.
    - Break the emotional bond to the old and create positive emotional ties to the new.
    - Give the fresh belief patterns a firm platform of existence in your life.

21. To flourish you need to replace old negative beliefs with those that are fresh, new, and original.

22. Don't be afraid to move ahead with bright, powerful, and courageous beliefs.

23. You have everything you need to be a huge success.

Chapter 3

LEARNING LIFE'S LESSONS

History is a great teacher. Though it has the capacity to
provide you lessons, leave it in the past where it belongs
and never allow it to overshadow the future.

I've been involved with success and abundance strategies for a long time, yet on occasions I still find the need to learn lessons, generally in times of uncertainty. In the past I quietly used them as excuses when I fell short of my objectives. In recent times, however, and in spite of the occasional pothole, I've come to a sound understanding of the channels via which I must travel and the metamorphoses through which I'm required to pass on my journey toward a wonderful destiny. It's an ongoing process of evolution.

Now more than ever, I clearly understand the need for lessons in life, although with experience I've become far more optimistic, grateful, and focused.

Life is brilliant; I have absolutely no doubt about that. It's imperative to research the answers to the pressing questions you face until you find plausible solutions and move through barriers. It's easy to make excuses for where you are at any given moment, as opposed to where you'd like to be. You may try to appease your guilt and frustration when you realize you are not achieving what you want. Those who sit on the sideline and watch the world pass by are the same people who complain about their situations when many around them make incredible strides toward their dreams.

> When you hear others speak of limitations in life, know unconditionally that, like the universe which cocoons you, there are no limits to the success and prosperity you can enjoy.

When you begin to work diligently and start realizing your goals, enthusiasm and newfound optimism subconsciously attract success and abundance into your life. It's a progressive journey and you must learn that effort is required to become successful. When it begins, stagnation will start to disappear. Each day we consciously build on our positive attitude as life continues forward with ever-increasing momentum.

Rather than make excuses for why you are not where you would like to be (it's that dream again, and nothing will *materialize* until you *actualize*), devise the plan and put in the effort which will take you to that desired destination. Once you realize you are actually achieving worthwhile milestones, your enthusiasm will kick in and fuel your drive.

> Out of immense struggle frequently comes the most monumental success. Those who have endured unbearable hardships are often the very same individuals who realize the greatest accomplishments.

I have at times found frustration in the initial stages of my journey. I watched many people around me moving forward while I pretended to be happy sitting in my shell, feeling disillusioned with my life, such as it was.

In reality I was unsatisfied and just a little envious of those who had the fast cars, celebrity friends, nice clothes, overseas holidays, fancy restaurant meals, and great houses.

Often it's difficult to watch others who appear to have everything in their lives while we seem to struggle just to possess the meager things of life. It doesn't seem fair—true enough. It can cause us to have a chip on our shoulder which we might never lose. It has the propensity to get bigger as we continue on this uneventful and obscure journey through life.

It's so easy to fall into the trap of self-pity. We wonder why the universe seems to smile on everyone else and not on us. "What have I done to deserve the hand I've been dealt?" I too once asked that question when I faced obstacles which I allowed to overwhelm me. I was putting in the effort (or so I thought); I was doing everything right and still nothing. I was working hard and being as nice a person as I could. I was dreaming of that better existence, but in reality my life seemed to be going nowhere. Why, why, why? The excuses began to flow as fast as the despair.

Without due appreciation and gratitude for what was in my life—rather than resentment for what was absent—the door to a colorful future remained shut; my scope and vision were narrow. My view of a bright and abundant destiny was severely impeded. The negativity was almost overwhelming.

It's times like this when you can easily become your own worst enemy, constantly feeding that tide of negativity which continues to rise around you. You may easily fall into that trap, because when you live with self-pity every day it can become a concrete part of your reality. It evolves into a ball and chain, constantly keeping you down.

> The past is simply a road map to your life ahead. Don't dwell on it, store it, or base your future on it. Learn lessons and develop a future established on those experiences.

Through negativity you begin to create that very reality you so much want to repel. The foreign entity you wish to resist will actually grow to be very much a part of who you are. It will become firmly entrenched in the negative thoughts and emotions you hold inside and project into every aspect of your daily life.

In the beginning of your awakening, the changes could happen slowly on some occasions and rapidly on others. When it really matters, you will see the obvious, and those shutters will open to an incredible, sun-drenched, colorful picture of what your future holds.

Once you apply yourself and add fuel to that fire and passion inside, the negativity should clear; you'll begin to see minute glimpses of what could be. Your dreams now have more clarity as construction begins on that awesome reality—the first step to realization. You'll know beyond doubt your wonderful life has begun.

On a number of occasions, however, you may unfortunately discover reality the hard way by falling back into old ways and listening to the detractors. This is counter-productive; it slows your progress, and if you continue on this path it will inevitably end in disappointment. Shut them out and move on positively.

> One of the greatest driving forces in life is the rejection we receive from others, often spawned out of jealousy and ignorance. Once we learn to harness the power within, we feed on the negative energy and begin to grow and succeed at whatever we do.

You cannot allow your quest to become a crutch—the endless pursuit of information, only to put it aside or lock it away without acting on it or putting it into action in your life. It should instead be used as a source of encouragement and support when you need a jolt or an injection of inspiration.

The fire of success that burns within must be the verve that fuels your dreams and visions of a better life. Understand that all the information in the world—the various CDs and DVDs, books, booklets, seminars, webinars, coaching sessions, and other self-help information on offer—will be worthless if you don't put it to good use building a great life for yourself.

You can attend countless sessions and buy all the related material as you ride on the tide of momentary euphoria. It's so easy to get caught up in the moment. It happens with monotonous regularity as you continue on your quest to find that elusive life you crave.

> Desperation and frustration are destructive and counter-productive elements of life, which thrive in dark places. Lose them and accept your innate ability to manifest great things through your dreams, visions, plans, and determination.

The speaker finishes; you have your "fix." Your heart and mind are full and the adrenaline is pumping. Spirits are high and the images of success and financial freedom flood like a tidal wave through your mind for those moments of true bliss as you leave the hall. You buy the supporting products and take your cache home, ready to begin the enlightened journey.

You guard it with your life and treat the material like a priceless heirloom. As hours become days, weeks, and months, your image of that brighter future begins to fade. The material remains on the shelf gathering dust. You have slowly but consistently lost the spark ignited by the power of the imagery created by the speaker and the information you ingested. Your visions of that incredibly prosperous future fade and you inevitably return to old habits.

You must rediscover the power and strength of your dreams, vision, and drive. Put what you've learned into practice as soon as possible before the spark is extinguished. Propel your life in the direction you know in your heart you need and want to move. Do it now without delay.

> Even on your darkest days, messages of strength can be found in your life. Listen intently, and each day put into practice all the tools which will see you seize every opportunity and embrace success.

Once you've received the material, sort through it with an objective mind. Work out what elements can immediately assist your journey. Once you understand the content and its relevance to your life, take steps to put all the information, strategies, plans, and programs into place. It's now time to begin the system of transformation before you lose the drive and passion.

Remember, it has taken your entire life to this moment to create your existing belief patterns. Your life's journey and all the experiences, thoughts, emotions, feelings, and encounters you've had to this point have developed the outlook you now possess. It stands to reason, therefore, it will take some time to deconstruct them and rebuild your future as a fresh and inspired place based on your renewed enthusiasm and drive and those innovative, inspired, and positive thought patterns.

> Time spent wondering "what if" is time and energy wasted. It could more easily be used to establish "what will be."

If you are truly focused and already have a plan in place, use the tactics you learn to fire your enthusiasm and push yourself to the next level of success. No matter how many seminars you attend or how much material you buy, it will remain a waste of money if you fail to put the principles into practice and begin the process of change today. You must learn all that life has the capacity to teach you and commit to positive action while the fire of enthusiasm burns brightly within.

Find the catalyst to move the clouds of apathy from your life. The power of prosperity resides within you, and when you learn to listen it has the capacity to fire your life in extraordinary ways. Realign your enthusiasm and reignite the power of your drive. Your mind will begin to absorb and comprehend all the information and advice you've received. Begin immediately to listen and act on the material or suffer the consequences of "*information fade.*"

When you allow yourself the freedom to stop and take notice of what's happening around you—to actually look, listen and comprehend the abundance of information available every second of the day—your mind opens automatically to so many more possibilities, which suddenly become endless. In those moments of inspiration, you'll find the courage and determination to contribute positively to conversations with your own well-constructed ideas and opinions, rather than paraphrasing the views and beliefs of others.

> I invite the sun to shine in my life every day and allow occasional clouds to
> form. They remind me just how powerful and fulfilling positive thinking and
> success are to me.

Fate is a wonderful companion and can't always be explained. You have
to be ready to receive the messages and be open to them, adopt the principles, and put your plan of action into place immediately. Synchronicity is an
incredible thing. It will assist you to open your eyes and, perhaps for the first
time, witness the endless opportunities and possibilities which are around you
every day.

Success is never as easy as simply closing your eyes and making a wish;
that's pure fantasy. It takes hard work and dedication. Irrespective of the
length of time that passes, don't allow feelings of desperation and frustration
to overtake you. You can't simply *hope* for a better life through magical manifestation and expect it to be instantly on your doorstep. You must work hard
and rationalize the probable outcome balanced against the effort you put into
your quest and the determination you have to succeed.

When these incredible opportunities arrive at your door, take them with
both hands. Be like a sponge with the priceless information at your fingertips.
Continue to soak it up and systematically apply it to your everyday life.

Always look for opportunities and tune in to the messages of optimism
you receive. Don't try and rely on luck, because I'm convinced you make your
own when your outlook brightens through an upbeat attitude, focus, determination, and gratitude. Give a wide berth to desperation and uncertainty. They
are the enemies of an optimistic outlook.

> Every path to success is littered with flowers which you must stop to smell
> along the way. You might stumble into the occasional pothole and have
> to navigate around obstacles to reach your ultimate goal. These are life's
> lessons; they allow us to savor the sweet taste of triumph.

I've long sought answers to endless questions in relation to success and prosperity and suffered ridicule at the hands (and words) of those who entertain neither an interest in nor an understanding of this incredibly revealing topic. These are the same individuals who move from day to day in a kind of twilight. They appear happy with their lot in life and seek no tangible answers to any pressing questions about who they really are and how and why they are at a given point in their lives at a particular time.

These individuals appear to shy from any form of challenge, which makes me doubt that they are happy with their everyday, uninspired lives. Nevertheless, I congratulate them on their apathetic and apparently happy outlook on life. I, however, have no desire to be in their shoes or walk the path they blithely tread. I'm convinced it would lead me nowhere and add no depth or quality to my life. One person's paradise can be another's prison.

> Success is not governed by color, sex, creed, age, or orientation. Success does not discriminate, nor does it know boundaries. It does, however, depend upon dreams, persistence, and self-belief. The moment you lose confidence in yourself, the shadow of failure will fall over your life.

To broaden your outlook on your future and enhance your opportunities, read widely and always ask questions. I did, and I uncovered some incredible information regarding the correlation between thought and reality and how we impact the equation.

Your questioning nature will lead you to uncover mentally and emotionally stimulating information. As you absorb the details, it will be as if someone is patiently shining a spotlight on the path ahead, making things much clearer for you. It will illuminate the darkness and make you much more positive and confident.

At this point, the need for recurring procrastination will diminish and you'll no longer have to hide your head in the sand. As you develop a sense of urgency in your quest for success, your attention becomes sharper. You begin to understand the true essence of your journey and the fundamental importance of focus and determination.

Lights begin to shine on all aspects of your existence as you commence that long and inspiring journey to quench your thirst for knowledge and improve your whole world in extraordinary ways.

At this point you understand success doesn't just *happen*. There's no magic wand or series of mystical words that can achieve total financial security. Realizing an abundant and prosperous life is not always an easy process, but it *is* possible and is certainly no secret.

> Don't rely on the enlightenment of others to show you the way. Use your personal light within to shine on the path ahead and forge your own strong and successful future according to your individual hierarchy of values.

To realize everything you want in and from your life, you must instigate real adjustments to your thinking, make positive moves toward aligning your actions with a successful mindset, and take every opportunity which presents itself in your life. As we begin to look for the good in every situation, no matter how overpowering it might at first appear, we should also learn valuable lessons from the various encounters and begin our search for appropriate solutions. This allows us to move forward with a renewed passion and purpose.

It's self-fulfilling because when we grow to be more positive in our entire outlook on life, we also become like magnets for wonderful things to materialize. Our lives become more balanced and much happier.

It was the positive, philosophical thinker James Allen who penned the immortal words, "All that a man achieves and all that he fails to achieve is the direct result of his own thoughts."[1] He also wrote, "Your thoughts and your dreams determine what you are and what you will be."

These powerful writings have as much relevance today as they undoubtedly had when Mr. Allen first put ink to paper and changed many of the then-mainstream misnomers on success and abundance.

It's imperative you build your life around your own dreams and desires and develop a strong, dedicated, and enthusiastic team upon whom you can rely for moral (and sometimes financial) support, information, and advice. A mentor can also guide you through the mire, but first you must make up your mind on the life you want and take the crucial action necessary to begin that chain reaction leading to success.

Simply thinking about something is just a wish. When you see it in your subconscious it's a dream; when you tell someone, it becomes a vision. When you act upon it and take real steps to achieve it with a plan of action and persistence, you have the capacity to change that dream into a reality and profoundly improve your life forever.

There is an old saying, "Fake it 'til you make it." I know so many people live their lives by this incongruity. It leads nowhere and sets you up for failure. In living this way, you're simply masking your existence in a false (fake) and negative reality.

When you spend so much of your precious time faking it, you don't actually develop the ability or momentum to capitalize on the vast every-day opportunities to make your future a very positive and abundant place. You will begin to accept this bogus and unsubstantiated state as your reality—a void—which will soon become the norm in your life. In many cases it brings some level of gratification and recognition but remains a total fabrication which can only lead to eventual disappointment. You're basically living a lie.

I live by another adage: "You'll see it when you believe it!" coined by the wonderful Dr. Wayne Dyer and the title of his very informative book.[2] It should be imprinted on the mind's eye of all who are serious about finding opportunity and embracing success.

Practice the art of seeing your bright and prosperous future in your mind's eye every day, and begin right now the process of making your dreams a reality.

The elusive door *can* and *does* open and allow you to step through to greater opportunities. Have faith and determination, but most of all keep alive your dream of a better life to fuel that fabulous plan of action. Know who you are, where you're going, and the means you'll use to get there. Capitalize on and be grateful for every opportunity which presents itself in your life.

> When people around you speak of what is impossible to achieve, use your success to quietly show them that their opinions are merely reflections of their own lack of self-belief.

Constant complaints about every little hiccup will see you miss opportunities. Incessant complaining and nit-picking is destructive to positive growth and development. Understand things happen for a purpose and take time to stop and see the lesson in the problem. You are destined to move on to greater things. One minor incident doesn't amount to a monumental mistake.

It's counterproductive to hold others responsible when things go wrong in your life. It's a natural, knee-jerk reaction to try and shift blame. However, when you stop and think you'll generally see the reason for the problem. The answer will also be at hand, and with positive and focused thought and soul-searching you can develop the right prognosis and piece together a functional and cohesive plan of action to give you an encouraging and often life-altering result.

> Never think of anything in life as impossible. Simply use the challenge as a yardstick against which to measure your dreams and evaluate your persistence.

Every problem has a solution, and every solution offers a new path forward. Be determined, driven, and focused. Remain positive and upbeat and hold in the forefront of your mind your vivid and colorful picture of the kind of future you know is within your grasp. Don't settle for less than you want and know you deserve. To do that would be to admit you are worth less than you truly are, and in doing so you render your life and your existence potentially worthless.

Don't stop working hard, even when you're eventually living the kind of life you want for yourself and your family. It will take effort to maintain the lifestyle you create. Never stop striving for the next great goal in your life.

It's this hunger which keeps you sharp and focused. Don't allow the new-found comfort to make you complacent, because it's a backward step and it will begin to erode all that you've built.

There is no end to the magnificent journey you're currently on as long as you maintain the focus and determination. Your life will just continue to improve in extraordinary ways.

NOTES

1. James Allen, *As a Man Thinketh* (New York, NY: Tribeca Books, 2011), 41.

2. Wayne W. Dyer, *You'll See It When You Believe It* (New York, NY: Quill, 2001).

Just because we may be traveling on the same plane doesn't mean we're taking the same journey. Build your itinerary around your own dreams and desires, using personal power and energy as your one true source of inspiration for achievement.

LESSONS LEARNED

1. Be grateful for obstacles encountered/lessons learned.

2. Constantly look for the silver lining in every dark cloud.

3. There's no magic potion for success.

4. Stop procrastinating and develop a sense of urgency in your quest for prosperity.

5. Success is not always an easy process, but it's certainly no secret!

6. Look, listen, learn, and contribute to your success through each contact every day.

7. Help and guidance come if you open your mind and heart.

8. When opportunities arise, accept them graciously and with both hands.

9. Problems are fated to be repeated until lessons are learned.

10. Success comes when you have adjustments to thinking and positive action.

11. A plan is crucial to a successful and abundant future.

12. Build your life around your individual plan/s for success.

13. Don't allow complacency to become the erosion factor.

14. The magnificent life you're leading need never end.

Chapter 4

COMMIT TO CHANGE

The instant I commit to positive change in my life, I begin
to evolve into the person I envisage myself becoming. The
degree of success I attract will depend upon my dreams,
determination, and the plan of action I put in place now.

When you make the true and unwavering commitment to be successful, it's at that defining moment you actually set in motion the wheels which begin the process of attracting greatness into your life. Until that time, you give power to indecision, doubt, and delay in and over your life. These are dark forces which reside in each and every one of us. They will surface and continue to interfere with our lives until we deny them influence over our positive thoughts and actions and truly begin the process of manifestation.

Many have learned to tap into that well of self-belief and push the negative influences out of contention in their quest to be the best they can using their skills, talent, dreams, determination, and passion to achieve everything they envisage in their lives.

A commitment to success and prosperity is akin to a relationship on the physical plane. We often ignore certain pointers, enjoying life such as it is with a degree of apathy and indifference, without actually looking beyond the here and now. We suddenly encounter a breakdown which takes us by surprise.

It happens so easily, and until we put a concrete plan into play and commit to a specific course of action, we won't begin to understand the power we have at our fingertips to improve life. It opens brand new windows, doors, corridors, pathways, and gateways.

Commitment to change pens the chapter on creating new relationships because with it comes those fresh opportunities. You begin to see life through bright eyes and a brand new and innovative attitude. Not all change is positive, but a clear idea of where you want to go in line with your dreams, visions, and that carefully conceived plan of action will lead to a positive, focused, and channeled transformation.

> Until you have the courage to take on more than you believe you can do, you won't ever know your true capabilities.

Commitment takes courage because it inevitably moves you out of your comfort zone and sometimes into potentially stressful and uncertain places. It requires effort and sacrifice. However, you can relieve this by being determined and driven and knowing beyond question exactly what it is you want. Constantly focus your full attention on the life you wish to follow.

As with any relationship, a real commitment to success principles removes the hesitancy you might have in terms of your total input to the actions required to achieve your goals. It becomes a pledge—a vow to incorporate a specific cluster of actions in your everyday world—which has the ability to change your life, stimulate your optimism, and push you in the direction you wish to go. The rewards are outstanding.

> For every goal you achieve, you should muster the courage and persistence to strive for another.

It's widely held that where there is commitment, ignorance and hesitation give way to a real knowing and the door is opened to providence. It reduces the possibility of ineffective behavior in the everyday pursuit of your dreams.

It's at this point many things begin to occur. Dedication throws open the window and allows the breezes of change and opportunity to blow freely and frequently through your world.

In these specific and positive actions, doors begin to open because you have a clear focus on where you are and where it is you want to be. Doubt and indecision have not been allowed to permeate and subsequently sabotage your plan of action.

You become attuned to the wonderful things which present themselves in your everyday life. You've begun to tend the fertile garden of truth and value in your life.

It's often at this defining moment you understand the power you have inside, your ability, and your capacity, which are enhanced through this one declaration you make to your life and your existence. The action frees you from many inherent constraints, and you begin to understand the power of the "self."

> Once you have the courage to step outside your comfort zone, you'll allow the breezes of freedom and success to fill your life.

Courage is a very specific tool. You will need it to make some commitments, especially those which appear to go against the grain of your set belief patterns.

From that one positive and results-driven action you begin to cast preconceived fears aside and display your boldness, determination, passion, drive, and focus. It signals your willingness to step out of the shadow of mediocrity into the warm light of opportunity. It empowers you with the confidence to move forward with renewed interest in your future. It enables you to shine from within.

Among the many powerful words written by Napoleon Hill are these, published after his death in 1971: "The absence of fear and not formal education or brilliance of mind is the major cause of success."[1] This very potent sentence sums up the tremendous power we all possess if only we can eliminate fear from our lives and tap into and trust our own true magnificence. We need to permit our personal light to shine on all aspects of our lives and begin to graciously accept setbacks as well as fulfilment.

Any day is a great time to change your life and attract that success into your world. You simply make the decision to do so.

If we recognize Napoleon Hill's empowering statement as fact, we also acknowledge it as a fundamental key, giving us the strength and courage to overcome any obstacles to the achievement of extraordinary things in our lives. It would stand to reason that the power of the mind is an untapped resource, enabling us to overcome fear in our quest for success and provide us with the power and ability to fully appreciate and embrace limitless abundance.

When we focus on the positive and infinite opportunities which abound in our lives every day, we are giving ourselves the green light to seek and embrace achievement. It's at this point we realize that the possibilities for prosperity become endless.

Mr. Hill was convinced that whatever adversity is faced in life—no matter what obstacles are put in our way; whatever problems, troubles, or failures we endure—there is an equally impacting benefit arising from that event. Eliminating fear gives us the power and freedom to turn adversity into advantage.

Don't wait until tomorrow to commit to your dreams, visions, and plans—to an abundant future, no matter how insignificant or unrealistic you may think it is (through your own innate doubts and often the insensitive and ill-informed words and actions of others). Trust in yourself; view life from a clear and unobscured vantage point.

Your dreams are your blueprints for the future. Believe in them totally. Embrace them and hold them to be the absolute truth of your existence. It's then you can begin to create your plan and fuel it with every positive aspect of your being.

Take the steps necessary to achieve everything you wish in life; the commitment launches your boat into a rapidly flowing sea of prosperity. Your self-belief and determination become your rudder and sail. Begin your inspired journey now. Without it you'll continue to flounder, and doubt will become your constant companion.

NOTE

1. Napoleon Hill, *You Can Work Your Own Miracles* (New York, NY: Fawcett Columbine, 1996), 60.

When we open our minds and hearts and ask for what
we truly want—when we remain focused and certain of
the ideal life we wish to live and fully embrace it—the
universe has an uncanny knack of giving it to us.

LESSONS LEARNED

1. Commitment sets in motion the process of attraction.

2. Indecision and doubt can have real and debilitating power in your life.

3. Commitment opens new pathways, corridors, and gateways.

4. The drive for success takes courage because it will remove you from your comfort zone.

5. Commitment eradicates hesitation.

6. Dedication reduces the possibility of ineffective behavior.

7. You require courage to be truly driven and pursue change.

8. Dedication puts into play a whole chain of positive actions.

9. Commitment engenders confidence.

10. Let your light shine; become accomplished and fulfilled.

11. Focus and determination begin an inspired journey to success.

Chapter 5

REMOVING THE ("GLASS") CEILING ON SUCCESS

When you tell yourself often enough that you're a fantastic person—worthy of great success and abundance in your life—and you believe that to be an absolute truth, success is inevitable.

To fully embrace success and be the very best you can, you need to understand what success and abundance are—how to attract them into your life and keep them as part of your core being. First, learn to develop a *wealth mindset* and, in that, refrain from applying an instant monetary (or specific tangible) value to everything you do.

You should not view success (wealth) solely in terms of the cash flow it will bring to your door—the new house, car, holidays, designer clothes, etc. Though these are important, they should not form the nucleus of your driving force. You must hold fast to the notion that you will derive deep and lasting satisfaction from your creativity, skills, and abilities.

> The seemingly impossible will forever remain an elusive dream, while ever you limit your imagination. The path to success is the unquestioned belief in your ability to be incredible.

No matter what line of work you're in you must add value to your product or service by attaching a price—that's separate from putting a ceiling on the value of your work. When you do, from that point everything you undertake—every action, word, thought, and emotion—automatically has a price tag attached. This act will give your creativity a ceiling—which becomes a limit. This automatically puts a lid on the worth of your work (and life).

Always believe your work and creativity hold vast promise and ongoing untapped value—truly priceless commodities worthy of enormous respect. Your thoughts, words, and actions must always support your dreams and goals, which will remain achievable as long as you continue to believe in yourself and refuse to succumb to the errant words and actions of others who, for some bizarre reason, might wish to steer you from your path.

When you allow the baggage of anger, procrastination, frustration, fear, and negativity to permeate your life, you're creating (invisible) chains which hold you back from achieving greatness. If aspects of the past don't assist your quest to push forward in the direction you wish to move, simply let go. Divest yourself of those anchors and choose not to follow that path.

Always believe in and be proud of yourself and your life. Know that whatever you undertake has real and tangible value, and there will be many people who want and need what you have to offer and are willing to pay you for it.

You should neither under-value nor under-estimate who you are or the power and value of your dreams, creativity, skills, experience, and ability. It is important you apply an initial value to specific items of work to ensure other people do not take advantage of your generosity, skills, or experience and that you receive a good return on your investment.

Accomplishment results from the unmistakable resolve of planning, action, and commitment.

Once you fully appreciate and support the value and understand the true worth of self-belief and determination, you will come to the realization that the very act of applying a ceiling and a limit on yourself has the capacity to render all your skills and experience less than they are worth. If you can apply an instant value to your life, then it automatically has diminished merit. It becomes simply a commodity which can be traded at that or any other price less than the true significance.

Believe beyond any question that your life is priceless. This includes your skills, experience, and creativity. Once you have this belief, you'll have a deep-seated appreciation of your true value as a person and an entrepreneur.

> When I stop worrying about who I am, I free myself to put effort and energy into who I can become.

There are exceptions to this rule, and I shall explain them to you. As an emerging coach and speaker (and indeed artist, business owner, tradesperson, or entrepreneur) you may find it difficult to initially secure clients. Many people are hesitant to sign up with or enlist the services of someone about whom they know very little, especially if they are being asked to pay for that service.

It's a great idea to offer a two-for-one consultation or add some other benefit where the client will receive the extended advantage of your skills and experience. In this way you can impart a great deal of your knowledge to that person or showcase your talent/products to a greater extent. This will invite clients to become familiar with you and your methods and pass your details to others in a networking process. In turn, you gain valuable experience and expand your client base, leading to greater financial freedom.

> When you understand the power of an unwavering belief in yourself and your skills, you will cease to worry about the ill-informed opinions of others.

This is important information for many individuals and businesses but more particular to speakers and coaches who might wish to package a variety of components in a cost-effective offer designed to tempt clients to join them and their mailing lists. The extended offer might include books, CDs, DVDs, booklets, downloads, and a variety of associated merchandise on top of any offer for discounted consultations.

Once you are established, however, there might be no need to continue this, although it is great to make these offers on an occasional basis. It serves to keep you and your services in the minds of clients and also assist in increasing sales. Word of mouth from satisfied clients is another great way to put your name in the public arena. It can, however, also work in reverse if your services prove to be below expectation.

These offers should be special and limited, principally to entice traffic to your door. You can also use the same method to give special holiday deals. This means that over the many international holiday periods, people can take advantage of your skills and experience at an attractive price. It can help to bring traffic to your door all year around.

As a client, it can prove lucrative for you to lock in to these deals, where you gain great assistance and guidance at a competitive price. The quality of the presentation and/or program is not diminished and you gain valuable assistance for a concession. It's a win/win situation.

We are what we want to be. Failure only finds its way into dark places.

You may be approached by a charity/organization with a request for assistance. While you are primarily a business and your goal is to make money and be successful, never underestimate the power of charity. First and foremost be grateful that you are in a position to assist and have been chosen as the person in whom the organization has faith.

I'm a strong advocate for support to charitable institutions—we all have our favorites—as it's great for the soul and can lead to even greater business rewards. Philanthropy is integral to success, but understand and respect your limits. You can afford to be selective and, above all, ensure you don't neglect your own family, friends, community, and business (and your plan).

In many ways, charity is a requirement for success, and when given in a very open and positive way it has a wonderful capacity to come back to you. In the act of giving, you release endorphins into your system. These are produced by the pituitary gland in times of excitement. They are fundamentally good components of our being which raise our consciousness, prick our senses, and leave us with general feelings of euphoria.

When we give to others without expectation, we allow ourselves in those moments to feel good about our actions. That's a benefit we should never deny ourselves and continue to embrace at every opportunity.

Even an extraordinary life can have an uneventful beginning.

When everything you do is geared toward receiving money or a payment of some kind, you still labor under the notion that it (money) is the one fundamentally important component of everything you do. We need money to live, and we must acquire reasonable funds to be as comfortable in our lives as we can; that's an inalienable right.

However, to instantly apply a blanket monetary value to your work, your creativity, or your personality and neglect giving any thought to the intrinsic value of each individual piece or action—or the true value of yourself as a creator, developer, or thinker—is to take away any identity or value those aspects of your being have. You render those characteristics of your life less than the valuable commodities they are.

For the next twenty-four hours, I shall love everything about myself, smile when I look into a mirror, and give myself the love and respect I deserve. Once I do it for that short period, I'll know I can do it forever.

I think of my work—my ideas, creativity, passion, vision, and the results of my efforts—as priceless wares. I enjoy every aspect of my job, and it's a joy to wake up every day and know the hours ahead are filled with life, color, clarity, depth, and drive through a variety of exciting projects.

First and foremost, you must love what you do and think of your work not simply as something being churned out on an assembly line but rather as creative, colorful, and wonderfully engaging works of art—no matter what it is you undertake—all the while developed with care, respect, and gratitude. It gives a deeper meaning and greater longevity to what you do.

Once you can learn to do this, you will have a renewed respect for and belief in yourself, both as a wonderful individual and a true success. The benefits of this action will have begun to flow in your favor, and you will be carried on your journey, as long as you don't lose sight of your dreams, goals, and emotions.

To do this gives you the drive to add real meaning to your life. It removes any ceiling you may have applied, directly or indirectly, to your achievements. Moreover, it gives you the true reason to get out of bed in the morning and work with purpose, confidence, and dedication in your journey to achieve those wonderful and worthwhile goals.

Financial freedom is a tremendous asset in life and can add depth and vitality to one's existence. It has the capacity to eliminate many difficulties, though it can also present a whole new set of problems of its own if you don't have the right attitude.

To achieve financial freedom, you must adopt the "millionaire mindset" and have unerring belief in your ability and capacity to achieve great things.

Throughout history, the number-one time-proven method to become a millionaire is to be a business creator/owner. Almost 75 percent of self-made millionaires have been those who have owned their own businesses, generally developed and nurtured from the ground up with determination and a great deal of effort, energy, and focus.

These luminaries include Andrew Carnegie, Henry Ford, J.P. Morgan, Bill Gates, Warren Buffet, Sir Richard Branson, Sheldon Adelson, Sam Walton, Jack Crawford Taylor, Larry Page, Sergey Brin, Dennis Tito, and many others with the vision and self-belief to create strong and successful business enterprises. They had a vision of the life they wanted and, with determination, set about creating something which would stand the test of time.

> When you are living a good and empowered life, ensure that you constantly praise yourself for what you do and the way you live.

Wealth can also be accumulated through becoming a high-achieving business executive, a successful salesperson, a specialist (such as a legal/medical practitioner, accountant, property investor, or business advisor), perhaps a creator/inventor, a highly-paid entertainer or sportsperson, or maybe via a windfall, the stock market, or an inheritance. The power of the Internet, too, offers immense opportunities to create wealth through clever application and dedication.

In the last fifty years, there has been a monumental shift from the expectation that a person will stay in one job until retirement. Many changes are occurring in the workplace through the impacting economic climate and continuing technological evolution. Boredom and frustration are now real challenges providing the impetus to go out and make more money.

The Internet also brings with it greater wealth-building possibilities through creating *additional streams of income* (ASI). This very important aspect of life is more fully outlined in Chapter 13.

There are so many avenues through which you can realize a dream of financial freedom if you apply yourself through the plan of action, fueled by determination, drive, and passion. Make up your mind to be financially free and set about putting the wheels of success into motion. You will realize that prosperity is well and truly within your grasp.

Your passion, drive, and unswerving commitment to success and abundance will surely turn each ordinary experience into an extraordinary memory.

Overall success, however, is not necessarily something material or a product on which one can put a price. It's certainly not like a new suit or a car. As a state of mind it has a value, true enough, though it can't be measured.

Success is a very real but often elusive entity that is truly possible for all of us at any time—provided we believe in ourselves and our talents and work systematically toward success, regardless of our circumstances.

Success is a state of being made up of various elements that give depth and meaning to the lives we live and the people we are and strive to be. It means something different to every person. What I strive for will differ from what you want, and therefore you have to seek your destiny through using your own tools and plans which you've streamlined to your own requirements.

There are two major blocks to success—fear and doubt. Fear of what has gone before and doubt about what's truly possible. Eliminate both and learn to embrace the reality of prosperity.

The way I go about seeking my abundant future will differ from the methods you use, although we will both embrace the fundamental tools of dreaming, planning, focusing, driving, and embracing. The results will of course differ depending upon our individual goals, visions, and wishes. The amount of effort you put in place will also differ from that which I apply. A great deal of it is based on determination and expectation.

Through the years I've heard myriad people speak of "the winds of change" which are blowing through life. I scarcely understood what was meant by this and have no doubt that those using the term also never fully understood the meaning of these wonderful words. The winds of change—both positive and negative—do truly blow constantly through our lives.

When we attune ourselves to the greatness around us, in some unexplained ways the positive winds can and do touch us. They feel like real breezes blowing through our homes and bringing vitality and energy to our lives. They freshen our very being and blow away the dead leaves that gather at our feet, the clouds from overhead, and the darkness from our minds. They help to make our worlds clear and alive.

> Always do what you can with the skills you have, based on the dreams you create, in the time at your disposal, to enrich your own life and the lives of those you love.

You can direct and influence these winds and the profound impact they can (and will) have on your life. Embrace their ability to change every aspect of your existence. By using your dreams and visions and a very positive attitude, attract the kind of winds you want to blow through your life and touch every aspect of your existence. Continue to be focused and committed and add zest and energy to the magnificent journey you're on. Your great future will unfold.

The value of commitment was aptly noted by Vince Lombardi, voted the NFL 1960s Man of the Decade and also Coach of the Century for his tireless work with several great American football teams, including the Green Bay Packers and Washington Redskins. Vince was quoted as saying, "The quality of a person's life is in direct proportion to their commitment to excellence, regardless of their chosen field of endeavor."[1]

Understand (and believe) that success is certainly within your grasp, no matter who you are or where you're from. The clouds of doubt and uncertainty will begin to lift from your life when you focus on your dreams and commit to your journey. In spite of the problems you encounter day to day, remain positive and focused and work conscientiously toward those goals. Success and abundance can and will happen in your life.

> Success is the ongoing accumulation of positive actions and interactions in our lives, which we practice daily.

A successful person need not have an over-abundance of material (and financial) wealth, which is only one aspect of this phenomenal state. The conditions are not co-dependent, though they are nonetheless often inextricably linked. The successful person is someone who is happy with who he/she is and where he/she is in life at any given time—a special someone in complete harmony with their work and the world around them. Everything they do has a positive and empowering impact on their society.

The successful person constantly adds ongoing value to their life and business by being totally focused on goals and consistently applying the principles of respect, balance, and harmony to the various personal development, wealth creation, and accumulation processes they instigate.

> The adoption of these very positive and driven procedures will herald the encouraging and consistent expansion of the overall value of your existence and an increase in personal wealth, if that is, in fact, what you seek (many simply seek greater harmony and balance).

There's absolutely no doubt that you can certainly become wealthy with the correct state of mind—*the wealth mindset*—a tangible and supported plan of action, and a commitment to an unshakable attitude of personal success and abundance. When you work hard with a positive outlook, opportunities come onto your radar and the future opens to you in all its splendor. Once again, they are rights and not privileges.

> Success should not become the pot of gold at the end of the rainbow—something which you pursue relentlessly in the hope of capturing it. Instead, it's something that should be attracted by the right mindset, planning, dreams, passion, and positive action.

Along with those rights come responsibilities—to yourself, your family, and those who are less fortunate. That encompasses the whole aspect of social conscience and adopting an attitude of free and unencumbered philanthropy to others.

When you expect certain things to occur, others can, in return, expect a certain standard of behavior from you. That means having respect and adopting a charitable mentality—having regard for those who do not possess the means or circumstances which you do and assisting accordingly. If you expect to receive in abundance, you must be prepared to give in the same way.

As you become this focused and driven individual, you will automatically begin the wonderful empowering action of systematically applying your skills, experience, drive, and determination to creating a lifestyle in keeping with your dreams and desires. *Nothing in life is unimaginable*!

NOTE

1. "Famous Quotes by Vince Lombardi," Vince Lombardi, 2010, Commitment, accessed June 12, 2014, http://www.vincelombardi.com/quotes.html.

Never underestimate the value of commitment and
never, ever equate success with mediocrity.

LESSONS LEARNED

1. Never put a monetary ceiling on yourself and your creativity.

2. Don't allow negativity from the past to hold you back.

3. Always love what you do.

4. Approach your work with care, respect, and gratitude.

5. There are many ways to derive income. Be creative and explore all avenues.

6. You cannot put a price on success.

7. Abundance is not measured strictly in terms of material wealth and/or money.

8. Success is a state of being; it adds depth and meaning to life.

9. A successful person is happy with life and in complete harmony with the world around them.

10. Success is truly within the grasp of all of us.

11. Along with rights come responsibilities.

12. One must adopt a charitable mentality and freely assist others.

13. As you become focused, driven, and committed, empowerment will follow.

Chapter 6

BEING THE BEST YOU CAN

You can never be the best at what you do until
you learn to appreciate yourself and your efforts
and do the best with what you have.

Though there are some exceptions, the majority of us strives to achieve the very best for ourselves and our families in everything we undertake. Irrespective of our backgrounds and in spite of the many positive and negative things that impact us in different ways every day, most of us carry this enduring thirst for success in some form through every aspect of our daily lives. The awesome untapped power of the human spirit prevails.

When we learn to embrace opportunity through understanding the incredible inner power we possess and begin to align ourselves with exactly the actions required to deliver what we want in our lives, we'll more easily increase our drive and determination and harness the limitless ability to make vast improvements in our everyday lives. We should never take this wonderful new existence for granted but be eternally grateful for every positive and empowering aspect of our lives.

Simply saying you want to be the best you can in your chosen field won't guarantee success. It remains a wish, residing some place in your subconscious.

Being the best requires some effort, which won't always come easily. It entails action and demands constant work to remain as a relevant force in your life.

Apply these principles to all aspects of your life. If you truly want to do and be the best in whatever you undertake, you must understand what's required if you want to stand out from the crowd. It takes thought, action, and vision, but the rewards are worth the effort. It requires a steely determination and an unerring belief in your own magnificence.

Those who strive to be the best and do their best are supreme optimists. They have a clear and powerful vision of where they want to be and entertain no doubt about their own relevance and importance. This is not arrogance but rather courage, determination, focus, and self-confidence.

The optimist has a supreme belief in his/her own strengths and abilities and knows the path they're traveling is right for their life journey. These motivated people—just like you and me—constantly strive to find better, more efficient, and more effective solutions to maintain a real edge in their everyday lives.

> When you're doing the best you can, it will be the time you are the best you can be. It's then that success will be knocking at your door.

Optimists are curious by nature and achieve great things in their lives because they constantly strive for greatness in all aspects of their existence. They have an unwavering belief that if things are not as they should be, they can and will improve. They constantly observe the world around them and have a clear and unobstructed vision of their future. They are generally ahead of the rest in their efforts to lead and achieve. Through a very real strength of character, optimists see the future in all its clarity and know their destiny is bright and filled with abundance.

No matter what others around you are achieving, you must believe beyond question that you too are capable of great things. When you show courage and determination in the face of adversity, you are exercising your deep strength of character and self-belief. This will reduce your fears and increase your ability to see opportunities as they arise in your daily life.

> While you continue to do your best and achieve great things even in the
> face of darkness and despair, there will always be opportunities to shine.

Never relinquish your high standards to please others. Always remain dedicated and focused; ignite your passion, vision, and desires through your own supported plan of action. Use your commitment and enthusiasm as beacons for others to follow.

You are a courageous and forthright individual. You have no need to seek out and embrace the skills, creativity, and dreams of someone else to make you whole. Each of us has everything inside to ignite the true flame of enlightenment. Instead of saying to another person, "Without you I would not be complete," practice instead the words, "You and I are a great team," or, "We complement each other perfectly." That's ideal synergy!

Others in our lives should only ever balance and match the skills we have, adding depth and clarity to our already rich and abundant lives, further enhancing our feelings of completeness.

> Give life and power to your dreams by constantly injecting them with clear
> and unambiguous vision, enthusiasm, persistence, and color. Never allow
> them to rest in the hands of another.

Live your life for yourself and never rely on the light of others in the mistaken belief it will assist you to somehow blossom and evolve. In your constant state of evolution, you are an incredibly special and complete individual, capable of creating richness and color in your own life without the need for the shadow (and the anchor) of someone else. Simply believe this to be so and have the courage to commit to change in your life for greatness and true abundance to begin.

Don't compromise your morality for the sake of a quick buck or consider accepting second best in any area of life. It displays a total disregard for your own principles and is a clear indication of your inability to embrace your own magnificence.

Through this negative action, you're actually indicating to others (and yourself) contempt for your dreams, visions, and goals. It displays a very real lack of self-respect that eventually leads nowhere and destroys the dreams and wishes you may have.

> Every dream I have of a wonderful and successful life continues to bring abundance into my existence because I am deserving of great things.

Experience has taught me a valuable lesson—life can at times be challenging, daunting, very difficult, and exigent, with seemingly no apparent path ahead or light to show the way (at that particular moment in time). Often by our own negative outlook on life and the actions we take in response to those views, we also affect the way others see life. This can and often does have very destructive results for those in our circle who interact with us on a daily basis. It also affects those in the workplace who rely on us for support and guidance.

The delightful and endearing spiritual leadership teacher, bestselling author, and lecturer Marianne Williamson put it so thoughtfully when she said, "As we let our own light shine, we unconsciously give other people permission to do the same. As we are liberated from our own fear, our presence automatically liberates others."[1]

Don't lose faith in yourself or your dream for an abundant life. To do so is to give in to failure and reduce your life to just another ordinary plane of existence. It's paramount you maintain an absolute belief in yourself, your life, and the vision you hold for your wonderful and prosperous future.

Individuals who constantly strive for excellence can see with clarity where they need to be and exactly what is required to remain firmly on top of the game. These focused and driven people can see their bright futures in every complimenting detail. They strive for an abundant future, although they are working in the here and now to create that ideal life. They always have the goal posts in sight and play toward that shining light.

> The road to success is not always paved with gold. Occasionally there are large and ugly obstacles which should serve to keep you focused. You must not lose your resolve.

There's a reason why a very small percentage of the population (believed to be about 2 percent) controls a huge percentage of the world's wealth (above 90 percent). Likewise, there's also a logical reason for the argument that if the world's wealth was redistributed evenly across the entire population, within a very short space of time it would largely be right back in the hands of the original 2 percent. It's called the *prosperity consciousness*. These people understand the science of prosperity and apply it to every aspect of their existence.

This is in contrast to those who have what's termed a *poverty consciousness*. Even if handed a million dollars, these individuals would see it disappear from their lives in a very short space of time. They have little idea of wealth creation, growth, and preservation. They will largely remain in a rut until they learn the art of building prosperity. Quite often, too, they are unaware of this flaw in their ability to improve their lives.

While the accepted definition of *wealthy* is yet to be clearly defined, those who have exceptional affluence understand the principles of attraction and accumulation. They have a real focus and determination. They are visionaries who live a life based on a platform of recognition—of the actions necessary to build wealth—with the determination to do what it takes to improve their lives.

> Procrastination, hesitation, and self-doubt are the enemies of success.

These driven individuals expect the best because they always give of their best. In every aspect of their pursuit of excellence, they put in the effort required and focus their thoughts and words on the prize. Commitment is one of their calling cards, and they accept nothing short of the best in everything they do.

When you're driven by desire, you automatically do your best to reach the goals you set yourself—daily, weekly, monthly, and yearly. Each is a milestone, and collectively they add up to a lifelong pursuit of personal and professional growth and development. This includes all aspects of spiritual, emotional, financial, intellectual, and relationship growth. Each is a vital component of the complete "self" whom you strive to be; it's indicative of the balance which the driven person sees and constantly works toward. Nothing in life happens by accident. Success is a right, true enough, but it represents a huge goal toward which you must constantly and consistently work.

Personal growth does not occur by coincidence. Like success, it's something you see, feel, taste, and experience with every fiber of your being, and it becomes a part of your everyday existence as you work tirelessly toward your goals. You have to live and breathe personal growth as an ongoing experience.

To be the best you can, absorb more. Read, listen, learn, and never tire of evolving. All you see, think, feel, hear, and experience becomes an integral component of who you are and your drive to be the very best.

> I never accept mediocrity and firmly believe that because I always do the best I can and focus on my goals, success will follow as a consequence.

You need not necessarily rise above everyone else in your field to be the best. You need only work to your full capacity with the skills, determination, and plan you have in place. Continue to make the best of each day, avail yourself of every opportunity, and be always grateful for each and every blessing you have in your life.

In the pursuit of excellence in whatever you undertake, you must understand there will be fierce competition, as others could see your rise as a threat to their position of prominence. You will be pushed relentlessly by yourself and those around you. As you move on with your wonderful life, you will learn and adopt methods and strategies to help you stay ahead of the competition. Remember, they will be right behind you.

> Continue to learn every day—you'll continue to grow every moment.

Healthy competition prevents the development of a lax attitude. It stops laziness and predictability creeping into the equation. Above all, it assists you to constantly evolve and pushes you to greater heights and even more incredible achievements with the resultant positive outcomes.

To be and do the best in and with your life, you must understand and embrace the value of competent leadership. To be a successful and vibrant principal, you need to develop the skills which will make others feel compelled to follow you through the good and bad times.

A good leader is not afraid of challenge or temporary setbacks. Great strides forward often develop from delays, when a brilliant leader recognizes opportunity in adversity and maintains the focus and determination to pursue personal and professional goals in spite of the obstacles faced.

> An effective leader is an inspired individual who makes sound decisions and forges the path for others to follow, often in the face of monumental adversity.

Great leaders display enormous courage and vision. They support and nurture their innate principles for the good of the organization, irrespective of obstacles faced. They will also remain accountable for their decisions.

A great leader sets an example for others to follow and, in that action, lays down a sound and positive path along which others are unafraid to travel, in spite of the challenges which could be faced. Inspired leaders understand the value of sound communication. They resist the urge to demean or overtly exert their authority on employees (more in Chapter 11: "Effective Communication"). It would label them as threatening and ineffective and impact negatively on the organization as a whole.

> Every time you open a door, open your mind, and every time you close a door, make sure you shut out prejudice, greed, intolerance, ignorance, and dishonesty.

Parents, too, are leaders and mentors. Effective communication teaches them the gentle art of persuasion (more in Chapter 12: "The Gentle Art of

Persuasion"). It's paramount that parents (teachers and coaches) be tactful, respectful, and flexible when dealing with children and young people so as not to alienate them or adversely impact their self-esteem or confidence.

Our children fill our lives with joy, faith, love, color, gratitude, and endless promise. It is, however, the way we respond to the challenge of teaching them the qualities of life that ultimately determines the success or otherwise of the path they travel.

> Life is full of bridges to new, unknown, and often uncharted destinations. Listen to the inner voice when determining which to cross and which to pass.

You become a more successful and secure principal when you develop the tools of sound leadership. It takes time, energy, and focus but when accomplished will make you more certain of the path you're following and give you the passion and confidence to support and encourage your team (and family) to strive for even greater rewards.

Make the whole process of successful leadership development a driving force within. It should become all-encompassing with the drive for you to further reach for and achieve your personal and professional goals across the broad spectrum of your life as a whole.

When inspired, you may not easily accept second best, although when it does occur, acknowledge it graciously, learn your lessons, and work even harder to achieve the top prize. This, too, is an important aspect of being a good leader. You must be gracious in (temporary) defeat.

In doing your best, you automatically step out of the shadows as you are touched by a degree of success. In those special moments, you indicate your intention to live a full and inspired life rather than sit back and watch with apathy as your future passes by. Continue to contribute and you will continue to receive.

To be the best means doing your best at everything you undertake. Don't tackle goals in anything other than a committed way. Your future depends upon your focused effort and to do anything less would be counter-productive.

Reach for the sky and give your goals 100 percent effort and attention until the job is completed. When you learn to prioritize, you'll understand the necessity for completion (see Chapter 14: "The Value of Effective Time Management").

Select your most important goal (written down), which you believe will have the greatest positive impact on your life and bear the most fruit. Apply your total energy and complete it as far as possible.

> You cannot underestimate the power of belief. Some of the greatest achievements in history have been made by those who found and held on to the courage to dream and believe.

Once you finish one task successfully, you move on to the next most important and continue this process. Remember that success involves big and small steps and they should all be done in order to ensure your journey remains on track, on time, and within view. There will also be times when you can combine steps or eliminate some that are only superficial or time consuming. This means applying a more consolidated effort and being focused and driven in your approach to those ever-present goals.

There will be times when you'll need to show great courage and discipline on your journey. Always keep your eye on the prize and retain faith in what you're doing. During those periods you may question your direction and the actions you're taking. There will also be moments when you really don't feel like doing certain things. This is the time when you apply additional focus and commitment to tasks —*a sense of urgency*—and approach your jobs with drive, passion, and determination. Monitor the time you commit to projects so you end with more positive and professional results.

Any successful journey involves sustained, positive action. In those instances of indecision, understand and appreciate the entirety of your journey.

Take that step back and look at your plan objectively (not an easy thing to do in the beginning). Make the readjustments to your attitude and maintain the discipline. You have to remain focused on your goal/s. Believe in everything you stand for and have faith in the steps you take to achieve the greatest results through being the best person you possibly can.

> While you continue to do your best and put all your energy into your successes—even though you may sometimes falter—what others might say about you can't hurt you and will amount to nothing at all.

If you stray from your objective, always remind yourself why you're working hard and maintaining your plan. Gently but firmly bring yourself back on track. Seek assistance and input if necessary from others (those with the skills, knowledge, ability, and belief) to keep you focused and on the right path.

As you complete each task, it's crucial you congratulate yourself on a job well done. It need only be small but nevertheless a celebration of your positive steps forward. Remember the reasons why you are on your journey and give yourself the accolades you deserve for achieving milestones.

Conversely, when you falter or hit a momentary hiccup in your plans, don't waste valuable time berating yourself or making your judgment a self-recriminating post mortem. Understand where you went wrong, take on board the lessons uncovered, and in spite of the challenges you face hold fast to the belief that you are moving in the right direction. Your acknowledgement will be your ideal guide.

Have confidence in your ability to build a team around you directly and indirectly. It can involve making contact with someone who has already been where you are traveling and is happy to assist with your odyssey. There will always be internal and external relationships which require constant nurturing.

> When you find the goodness in others and acknowledge it with gratitude and respect, you'll discover the ability to find, acknowledge, and capitalize on your own monumental skills.

When you learn to have faith in those around you and give them the respect they deserve, you will begin to create and maintain lasting relationships. This builds a bridge between you and your contacts; you'll gain their trust and respect, and they in turn will be happy to be a part of your wonderful voyage.

The buck always stops with you. Acknowledge problems, accept responsibility, and make necessary adjustments to your plan, your thinking, and your approach, and then move on. Each time you get knocked down, get back up, dust yourself off, and pick up the ball no matter how difficult it seems at the time. It's far easier to chip away at the wall and even walk around it than to try to head butt your way through it.

What you *do* in these moments will have a much greater and longer lasting impact than anything you can *say*. Words can be hollow; positive actions are tangible and visible. Don't make excuses for what goes wrong in your life. You are the captain of your own ship and must therefore show the courage of your convictions and accept responsibility for your actions.

If you truly want to be the best you can, take stock of who you are and the qualities you possess. Enhance your existing skills and develop others. Know what you want to do and be courageous in everything you undertake. Be a compassionate, driven, and dependable leader.

You only have one life—live it to the full, with courage and determination, leaving a legacy for others to follow. Your light will continue to shine long after you've passed into history.

It's the quality of your actions and not the quantity of your achievements that leaves a lasting impression. When you strive to do your best, you present a bright and engaging canvas for others to use as a template for greatness in their own lives.

Effective leadership is about courage and love for the self and others in a true spirit of generosity and gratitude.

Don't always look for the easy way out, but rather do the best you can for yourself (and others) with the skills, drive, passion, and persistence you have and are rapidly acquiring. It's never about what others can do for you. It must always be about what you can do for yourself and others.

When you move into that head space you will begin to develop a courageous and optimistic attitude which will serve you as you proceed enthusiastically toward your wonderful future. Your light and compassion will be reciprocated.

NOTE

1. Marianne Williamson, *A Return to Love* (New York, NY: HarperCollins, 1992).

A business is only as successful as its people. Therefore, if you are your own business and you wish to embrace abundance, you need to think, feel, and be the best you can and surround yourself with empowered people.

LESSONS LEARNED

1. It takes real effort to be the best you possibly can.

2. Never take your new and empowered existence for granted.

3. Be grateful for every positive and empowering aspect of life.

4. Life can at times be challenging.

5. Be an optimist and know beyond question where you're going.

6. Weave excellence into the fabric of everything you do.

7. Set personal and professional goals and treat the achievement as a milestone.

8. Always embrace learning.

9. Welcome competition and use it to your advantage.

10. Competent leadership is integral to being the best you can.

11. Our children are precious; give them the tools to succeed.

12. Never overshadow young people with your own prejudices.

13. Don't try to live your life through your children.

14. Prioritize your goals with your full and complete attention.

15. Be committed and focused. Work with a sense of urgency.

16. Never fear asking for help.

17. Accept responsibility for errors, learn lessons, and move on.

18. Understand and appreciate your own wonderful qualities.

19. Don't rely on others to make you complete.

20. Enhance existing qualities and develop others.

21. Give yourself permission to shine.

22. Have courage and compassion in all you undertake.

23. When you do your best for yourself, your actions will mark you as an achiever.

Chapter 7

THE AWESOME POWER OF TRANSFORMATIONAL CHANGE

The instant I open the window to my destiny and allow
the cool breezes of optimism and opportunity to blow
through my life, I have the capacity to change my existence
to one of profound confidence and happiness.

The idea of *transformational change* is often considered quite radical and can require courage and a shift in assumptions about the organization and people. It can take place on both the personal and professional fronts. It comes about when the leader displays a true strength and courage in spite of the many uncertainties. This individual shows real leadership qualities in stepping out of the ever-present comfort zone in the face of adversity, and they apply innovative techniques—when necessary, with assistance from a specialist change agent. This is often done with a degree of collaboration necessary to have others share in the vision.

Transformational change is fundamentally an influential tool. It has the power to add a new enthusiasm to an organization through encouraging its people to look at work practices in a new and groundbreaking light. When applied correctly, it has the ability to create a buzz and unleash an enriched passion from which a new company image, a much brighter outlook, and more empowered and enthusiastic staff often result.

> When I freely release myself from the need for something debilitating in my life, I open myself to new and profound change.

It's no secret that a strong and inspired leader has the ability to take a company to incredible heights and achieve monumental goals. In my experience, staff will follow a leader with vision and passion in spite of the often hazardous and uncharted journey ahead.

A strong and effective leader has an innate integrity and displays a very caring and compassionate attitude toward staff and the business as a whole in spite of many impacting issues which can be faced on a daily basis. The empowering manager nurtures great empathy for the beliefs and opinions of others and openly displays all those fundamental traits which identify him/her as a courageous proponent of transformational change—a powerful concept designed to assist the business and staff members to grow and adapt as the company evolves.

Transformational leadership is a term first coined in 1978 by James MacGregor Burns. He was an eminent authority on leadership studies, a presidential biographer, and Woodrow Wilson Professor (Emeritus) of Political Science. Mr. Burns was also a 1971 Pulitzer Prize and National Book Award recipient for his incisive work, *Roosevelt: Soldier of Freedom 1940-1945.*[1]

> The choices you make today, which have the propensity to change your life, ultimately become your destiny play-makers. Therefore, ensure they're based on sound judgment, due diligence, and vision.

Mr. Burns asserted that transformational leadership occurs when individuals engage to an extent where all team members, irrespective of their place in the group, are capable of raising one another to higher levels. His work found that through a program of collaboration and the instigation of ethical and visionary leadership, people are capable of being elevated to a much higher and more productive plane.

Transformational leadership is a process of evolution through which the workforce is systematically *transformed*. The leader's passion and drive become infectious and enhance the morale and performance of the group through consistently motivating and leading with purpose.

Despite the scary name, transformational change in effect empowers individuals and corporations to convert their thinking and reinvent themselves and their approach to life. It enables those involved to see the bigger picture and understand how their behavior has specific consequences.

With a monumental shift in mindset and a willingness to step outside of their comfort zones, individuals can gain a new perspective on themselves and their lives, renew enthusiasm, and add drive and purpose to their thoughts and actions. This has the capacity to establish a greater quality of life and re-align the work/life balance.

> A great leader is one who shows courage, empathy, vision, and determination in the face of adversity.

According to Bernard M. Bass (Ph.D.), the Distinguished Professor (Emeritus) of Organizational Behavior at Binghamton University in New York, there are four fundamental elements in the makeup of the successful transformational leader:[2]

Role Model

Leaders are respected and trusted. They provide a clear vision with stated values and purpose, which gives meaning to the organization. Through vision and enthusiasm, the leader inspires feelings of pride and purpose in the team members (and/or stakeholders). This action in turn enhances performance potential. Even during those times where the leader is not present, staff members continue to show trust by emulating the behavior of the leader, readily identifiable through achievement of pronounced goals.

Show Consideration

This highlights a leader's ability to identify with the needs and feelings of individual team members. The leader acts as a mentor and coach, consistently challenging thinking and readily addressing, with empathy and consideration, any concerns voiced. The effective transformational leader always supports and encourages staff through this beneficial collaboration process. It gives power to the individual who seeks job satisfaction and craves constant incentive from their position in the organization.

Stimulation

The leader freely seeks input and ideas from staff/supporters, takes risks, and challenges long held assumptions. This action serves to excite and encourage the creative process in all personnel involved and gives them a feeling of belonging and contributing to the overall process.

The transformational leader will seek to stimulate and support individual creativity and encourage those who display independent thinking. All unexpected situations and obstacles suddenly become tangible opportunities to evolve. This behavior encourages followers to think laterally about situations, manifest plausible solutions, and in turn ask impacting questions. It encourages managers, followers, and staff to interact more fully and become actively involved in the growth and evolution process.

Motivation

This is largely determined by the degree to which the leader articulates a vision. It involves clear and effective communication as a fundamental tool to make the vision powerful and impacting. The leader generates and maintains optimism in relation to goals and gives real meaning to the task at hand.

Followers require a strong sense of purpose if they are to be motivated to act. They must be capable of identifying the meaning within the vision, which provides the verve and drive to push forward. When suitably motivated with a clear path and purpose, staff members (and/or stakeholders) readily identify with stated goals and become more optimistic and enthusiastic about the journey ahead with the drive to invest more time and energy to achieve them. Once followers can identify with the vision, the goals become clear and optimism and enthusiasm grow and flourish.

> Change will only be effective when you realize it is necessary in your life and you take the essential steps to embrace it.

To do this, the leadership must be willing to instigate the process of change. It many cases it will be necessary to alter and quite often expand the mindset of staff to readily embrace fresh and novel ideas. This is not always an easy task because there can be resistance to change.

However, once the management team and staff realize the necessity to lose the complacency and apply bright and modern thinking to their practices to improve their situations, they have the ability to discover functional and workable solutions to problems. This results in more positive shifts in attitudes, outlooks, and perspectives.

According to Gary A. Yukl, Professor of Management at New York State University (Albany) and the author of ten books on management, there are five tips for the successful implementation of transformational leadership.[3] The effective leader should:

1. Learn to involve employees and encourage their input in the development of an attractive though perhaps challenging vision.

2. Understand the necessity to tie the vision to a plausible achievement strategy for a successful implementation.

3. Specify the vision and translate it to action once it has been developed.

4. Be optimistic about the vision. Be decisive and express confidence in relation to the overall implementation.

5.   Understand the development process. It can take time, and therefore small successes should be valued along the way.[1]

I have instigated permanent and positive change in my life, because I have a clear and vivid picture of the wonderful direction in which my future is accompanying me.

Transformational leaders must display an aura of trustworthiness as they begin the process of selling their vision to others who at first, understandably, might be reluctant to follow (sometimes into the unknown). While the leader may have a clear and unimpeded vision of the direction they wish to go, others may not. This will create an atmosphere of insecurity with many.

In spite of the often radical nature of the change envisaged, the transformational leader will use every opportunity to articulate the value of the vision and use all tools at their disposal to assist in the climb.

These inspired individuals use their commitment to the concept of positive change to encourage a very real shift in thinking. It creates a vibe—a passion—across a broad spectrum of life, resulting in renewed creativity and enthusiasm. This in turn will add fresh excitement, depth, and color to the personal and professional lives of those who take up the challenge and adapt. It results in a more positive and regenerated focus on life.

An effective and competent leader utilizes the innate ability to motivate staff to rise to challenges, overcome adversity, and find the power within to achieve extraordinary goals, often in the face of overwhelming odds.

The empowered leader remains optimistic in spite of obstacles and constantly motivates so others don't lose faith in the vision which might not at first be obvious. He/she keeps the vision alive by developing appropriate strategies to support the vision and maintain enthusiasm for the journey ahead.

The realization that you have everything within to build the ideal life is a true awakening. You are an incredibly powerful being in your own right, irrespective of the life you currently lead. Once you take ownership of your life and begin the process of steering it to the horizon, you will begin to resonate.

NOTES

1. James MacGregor Burns, http://www2.fcsh.unl.pt/docentes/luisrodrigues/textos/lideran%C3%A7a.pdf

2. Bernard M. Bass (Ph.D.), www.changeminds.org/disciplines/leadership/theories/bass_transformational

3. Gary Yukl, "An Evaluation of Conceptual Weaknesses in Transformational and Charismatic Leadership Theories," The Leadership Quarterly 10, no. 2 (1999): 285-305, doi:10.1016/S1048-9843(99)00013-2.

I am unafraid of change because, when manifested by me, it becomes an open window through which blow new opportunities and an abundance of success and happiness for those in my life.

LESSONS LEARNED

1. Strong and inspired leaders can assist others to reach incredible heights.

2. Successful leaders display compassion and empathy for the beliefs and opinions of others.

3. Transformational leadership allows all team members to achieve higher goals through collaboration.

4. Transformational leadership transforms the workplace through passion and a shared vision.

5. Effective leaders are caring and compassionate.

6. Transformational leadership encourages companies and individuals to reinvent themselves.

7. There are four elements to a successful transformational leader:
   - Role model
   - Show consideration
   - Stimulation
   - Motivation

8. Transformational change empowers individuals.

9. Transformational change is an influential tool.

10. Transformational leaders sell their vision through passion, enthusiasm, and integrity.

11. Effective leaders constantly develop functional strategies to illuminate their visions and empower staff and others.

Chapter 8

TAKING CARE OF YOUR HEALTH AND FITNESS

Always be positive when setting your goals. Live in the here and now. "I am truly healthy and abundantly successful. My life is full to overflowing with love, happiness, wealth, good health, and abundance." Watch as your life transforms.

Being the best you can also means paying attention to your health and fitness—respecting yourself and your life. It is difficult to remain mentally alert when your health is not as good as it could and should be. In neglecting your wellbeing, you're denying yourself the opportunity to live a full and abundant life where you can make balanced decisions to ensure all aspects of your world are in harmony.

If you are not in reasonably good physical condition, you may be unable to enjoy the full extent of your success or sustain the maximum effort required to pursue your plan of action. This will impact your overall feelings of wellbeing and your ability to build wealth across all aspects of your life. Your self-esteem and feelings of self-worth will be severely impaired when you are unable to function at your optimum through a lack of stamina. You will be unable to achieve everything you would otherwise be capable of realizing.

Every day the abundance of power, success, and good health continues to grow exponentially in my life as I open myself to the wonder and enlightenment of the universe.

Maintaining optimum health and fitness doesn't mean you have to run ten kilometers each day, nor does it entail eating a vegan diet (though I applaud anyone who does either of these things; it shows enormous discipline).

When you are looking after your health, you are eating well, getting reasonable daily exercise, and refraining from those things which impact negatively on your quality of life. You are also clearing your mind through regular periods of meditation, having good rest and relaxation, and generally taking the time to listen to your body and respond accordingly.

When you enjoy good health and vitality, you literally resonate with great color and energy. You shine with overall wellbeing. Energy levels increase and you have clarity of thinking. In this way, you become more attuned to your environment and are better able to handle problems which arise. You also have the drive and focus to see plans through to their fruition.

Age can never be used as a barrier to success for with age come wisdom, knowledge, patience, love, courage, compassion, and generosity. These are the building blocks of abundance.

As age encroaches, it doesn't mean you automatically succumb to the ravages of ill-health, which can occur at any time during your life if you fail to take care of yourself. You should invest in regular check-ups to ensure you maintain optimum health and well-being to support success and happiness in your life.

We never think twice about the service on our vehicles, yet we avoid the visit to the doctor for many reasons. We never seem to have the time, or we have some unsubstantiated fear of a negative result. A regular check-up can arrest current medical issues and avoid future problems.

> Good health is a key to success, for without it you will be unable to truly savor the pleasure of your abundance.

If you don't enjoy good health and as a consequence are unable to apply yourself completely to your plan, it can seriously impact your capacity to create wealth. It will hinder your drive to continue when things get tough. You may lack the strength and endurance when the uphill motion becomes challenging.

Ill-health will adversely impact relationships—there's no argument about that. You run the risk of losing contact with much of the goodness which comes through your daily connection with others and the great opportunities which abound in your life. It adversely affects your ability to focus on the wonderful people and moments flooding into your life every second of the day.

An integral part of the recipe for success is the maintenance of your energy. A sensible diet and exercise regime expresses your desire to lead a fit and healthy existence and function at your peak.

> The word never is a negative, which should only ever accompany other negatives. These include poverty, sadness, ill-health, pain, loneliness, mediocrity, despair, and unhappiness. Remember that two negatives make a positive.

Success is something on which you must constantly work. It certainly doesn't happen by accident, and once you have success within your grasp you must systematically maintain the focus and commitment to continue.

Staying healthy and reasonably fit allows you to keep the fingers of oppression at bay and focus your mind and energy firmly on the horizon ahead where your destiny lies. You are able to work harder and for longer, with much more enthusiasm, determination, and vitality. You'll have greater focus and clarity in your life and be far better equipped to handle difficult situations.

I recommend you have regular check-ups and speak to your health-care practitioner about any health concerns you may have. Be guided by sensible professional advice.

If there is imbalance or inconsistency in any aspect of your health, take the necessary steps to rectify the problem. Prevent it from becoming a major issue by ensuring you take good care of yourself and seek medical advice whenever necessary.

> Rather than search for reasons why you can't be healthy, you should concentrate on the reasons why good health can and will assist in your journey to success and abundance.

Exercise your mind to be in perfect harmony with your body. Read extensively on a variety of topics (if only to broaden your knowledge and vocabulary) and meditate every day.

Meditation is better performed in a place of solitude where there are no interruptions. In time and with practice you learn to more easily fall into a full contemplative state, and in a very short space of time you'll enjoy the superb benefits of total relaxation.

> I strongly suggest, if you wish to embrace success and abundance in your life but labor under a stagnant and sluggish lifestyle, seek the assistance of a healthcare professional today and begin the journey to optimum health. It's something you can't afford to delay if you want to improve your life.

Meditation is certainly not some "new age" fad enjoyed by a closeted minority. That quiet, introspective time is an ancient method to improve overall mental health and vitality. Every leader and success coach practices some form of meditation. It's another crucial tool for personal and professional improvement.

> While you try to convince yourself that maintaining good health and vitality is too much of a struggle, you are in effect communicating to the universe your love of failure and mediocrity.

There's no better time to clear the baggage from your world. Begin the process of attracting great things into your life right now. It won't always be easy, but the results will amaze you when your future becomes crystal clear and the blocks to abundance begin to fall away.

I am grateful for my optimum health and the
happiness and abundance currently in my life.

LESSONS LEARNED

1. To be successful you must also look after your health.

2. Good health means sensible exercise, diet, rest, and relaxation.

3. Good health also includes your mental state.

4. Meditation is a time tested method to improve overall mental health and vitality.

5. Ill-health will impact your ability to create wealth.

6. You must constantly work on your success.

7. Success doesn't happen by accident.

8. Stay fit and healthy to keep your eye on the prize.

9. If you have any health concerns, seek professional advice.

10. Take positive and sensible steps to rectify imbalance and inconsistencies in your life.

11. Good health and vitality will help to remove the blocks to success.

Chapter 9

DEVELOP A CLEAR AND SUPPORTED PLAN OF ACTION

Your canvas of life will be with you forever. Therefore, you must carefully plan before you begin so you know just what it is you are creating. Always paint from the heart with love, gratitude, faith, and optimism. Use vivid colors, broad brush strokes, and above all take your time to ensure you create exactly the future you want.

There is a terrific saying which has stood the test of time. According to John L. Beckley: an American author and businessman and founder of the Economic Press Inc., "People don't plan to fail. They fail to plan!"[1]

In that lies the story of many otherwise successful people (and projects) throughout history. In their failure to plan they faced almost certain disappointment and defeat in an otherwise ideal market, often in spite of tremendous energy and endless cash poured into a brilliant product/idea/enterprise/service. Great ideas require endless attention and a positive approach.

According to the US Small Business Administration (2008), almost two thirds of new business enterprises survive at least two years while up to forty four percent survive at least four years.[2] Although this is a far cry from the long-held belief that fifty percent of businesses fail in the first year and ninety-five percent fail within five years, it is nevertheless a worrying figure.

Never feel shame if you strive yet fail to be the best at what you do. Instead, simply strive to do your very best at whatever you undertake.

Problems will arise in almost all aspects of your development. They can infiltrate your dreams, feelings, and emotions with profound effect if you allow them to have that power. Their impact often lingers for some time.

No matter what occurs in your life, you must believe your problems are only fleeting and success is your birthright. To some degree, through proper planning and a positive approach to all aspects of your life you can have control over the number and intensity of the obstacles you face.

Having a plan; being positive, focused, and determined; and remaining upbeat will reduce the intensity and longevity of any problem which impacts you.

Momentary failure is not the end of a commitment and should never preclude you from trying again. Take a deep breath, lose the self-pity and blame game, alter your plan, accept new and innovative approaches, ask for assistance, and if necessary adopt a more positive and upbeat state of mind.

If you keep doing things with the same mindset, using the same plan of action, and treading the same path, the result will inevitably be the same. If you want a different outcome, do things in a different way.

A plan of action is a platform upon which to create a strong and plausible framework of success. It helps steer all aspects of your precious life through the heavy sea, the rapids, and the often malignant storms into the calm and inviting waters of eventual prosperity and abundance.

You rarely leave home without knowing your destination, the route you'll take, and what you'll do when you arrive. Similarly, you should not contemplate a course of action without reflecting on the possible/probable outcomes.

If you never exhibit enthusiasm for what you do, you won't find the drive to get out of bed every morning with energy and focus and open the window to success and opportunity.

Don't be afraid to ask for assistance from others. When it comes, don't forget to express your gratitude for the good deeds done. Those (whom you trust) in a position to assist and who possess the drive and inclination to offer that helping hand should be welcomed into your circle and their information and advice embraced and absorbed.

Commencing a business or new venture or indeed starting out in any capacity without a decisive plan of action is akin to taking a boat out on the open sea without an oar. The journey might initially appear peaceful and extremely exciting, but time will show you have next to no chance of reaching your destination as fear and trepidation set in and you have to weather the various storms which arrive.

Without that plan your journey has no real momentum or direction, and you'll soon discover you have no ability to maintain effective control through the varied situations you'll encounter.

Every affirmative action you take or even consider generally has a purpose, normally designed to deliver a tangible result through a real and optimistic response and ultimately assist with positive growth and development.

If you constantly fight negativity, it will gain greater power in and over your life. When an obstacle presents itself, rather than continue to battle it simply acknowledge it and be grateful for the encounter. Disempower the negativity by making the choice to move on to something better. Replace it with a positive thought.

In general terms, none of us ever sets out to deliberately instigate an action which is counter-productive to our deep desire for achievement, nor do we set out to arrive at a destination where we don't wish to be. Living life to the full is a normal human yearning and means taking affirmative action to reach a desired objective, enabling us to derive enormous pleasure from the life we truly want.

Remember too, obstacles present themselves in your life to help you adjust your thinking and redirect your energy in a new and more supportive situation. It was Bruce Lee (martial artist, actor, and author) who wrote the memorable words, "Defeat is...a state of mind. No one is ever defeated until defeat has been accepted as a reality. ...Defeat simply tells me that something is wrong in my doing; it is a path leading to success and truth."[3]

Embracing life's purpose is at the very core of success and abundance. This might sound easy at face value, but often we drift almost aimlessly from one idea to another, searching for that single thing we believe will make us money, bring fame, and deliver a lifestyle we crave. It satisfies that inner hunger to achieve something greater than we already have.

Remember to always record those notions, ideas, thoughts, and theories in your journal. Some might not be perfect for that particular moment in time, but they could prove to be of enormous benefit in the future. They come to you for a purpose—don't discard them.

> My life is a platform for the development of excellence—a place where I find my true purpose and set about the task of success through dreams, visions, actions, and persistence.

Discover what truly drives you—that special something which ignites the fire within, giving your life meaning and direction. It's that very thing which fills your world with warmth and passion and empowers you to strive for even higher achievements. It must be in total harmony with your highest values—the list of those many aspects which have importance in your life, ranked highest to lowest. They are what inspire and empower us all to achieve great things (in spite of the obstacles).

Do you feel something missing from your existence? A void in your life which is difficult to fill, a yearning which pulls at your heart and impacts your wishes? Your purpose represents that aspect of growth and development identified as a vital component reflecting your dreams, passions, talents, and desires. Develop your plan around that principle of purpose.

> A change of destination without clear direction can take a lifetime to realize. A change in direction, however, is something which can be achieved overnight. Make it now and allow it to lead you to your amazing new destination.

Your life and the associated thoughts, words, and actions should always reflect what is important to you. Create something which gives you a reason to feel good about yourself and your existence. Your plan will reflect your intention, and in that lies your reason for continuing the hard work and determination as you move in your current direction.

When you understand your true function in life and are enriched by that very purpose, you have a wonderful foundation for your plan with far greater stability, depth, and direction.

Don't feel any shame or embarrassment in momentarily succumbing to setbacks when in pursuit of excellence. They occur for a variety of valid reasons. Learn from them, recognize them for what they are, and embrace the need for change.

Never shrink from the possibility of a challenge or confrontation when defending yourself and your plan of action. It will occur more than once. Embrace the opportunity because the experience serves to push you in the right direction. Your ability to defend your position and articulate confidently the positive attributes of your plan with a clear and unhindered vision will strengthen your resolve and make you more determined to achieve your goals.

The great Henry Ford (founder of the Ford Motor Company) said it perfectly: "Failure is only the opportunity more intelligently to begin again."[4] You learn the lesson, think of alternatives, and without any procrastination or a great deal of deliberation move forward with a far greater determination to succeed.

> When things seem to go wrong and unforeseen obstacles are suddenly thrust at you, simply smile, take a deep breath, and say, "I know I'm on the edge of something fantastic." Challenges are sent to keep us on track and remind us to stay focused on success.

Far too often we make excuses when things get difficult and we find ourselves moving against the traffic. It can be an automatic response as we surrender and accept the simple path rather than put our shoulders to the wheel and apply some effort to creating the ideal life.

The path is not always tranquil, but the task is made easier when we understand and embrace the reasons why we are traveling the path we're on and refuse to allow the obstacles to keep us down.

The very gifted Mark Twain, a writer, satirist and lecturer, once said, "There are a thousand excuses for every failure but never a good reason."[5]

Rather than wasting time thinking of all the excuses why you can't do certain things as the world blithely passes by, stand up, open your eyes, clear your mind, and begin thinking of reasons why you can.

You'll find literally thousands of both. The first might be easier, but the second will be far more exhilarating and worthwhile.

There is no such thing as a valid excuse to set your dreams and goals aside. If you can dream it, you can manifest that dream into a reality. Don't procrastinate; be positive and powerful.

If you want to experience success in your life, the fundamental rule of thumb is to embrace accountability. Build on the dream you develop for a better existence and brighter future with a clear and unambiguous plan of action.

> Never be dissuaded by temporary setbacks. Find that link; that sense of purpose for doing the things which are important in your life, and be determined to follow them through to their conclusion.

Understand that all thoughts, words, and actions have consequences. Be responsible for them at all times.

To accept accountability as an integral component of life, you must also be prepared to embrace responsibility. Understand why you do certain things and the subsequent impact your actions are having (and will have) on your future and the future of others. Clearly understand your personal and professional needs and link with them. Begin the process of planning for your future by putting a determined effort into achieving what's most important in your life.

Check that everything you do is positive, designed to deliver a very optimistic and empowering result. Protect yourself by being determined to do the very best you can—for yourself.

> Ensure you always see light where others see darkness, a rainbow where others see only clouds, and a yellow brick road where many might see only a dirt track overgrown with weeds and thorns.

Work optimistically toward your goals and dreams with courage, purpose, and determination. Ensure everything you do is enthusiastically charged and passionately executed.

Develop your plan in a step-by-step fashion to make sure, as best you can, that you cover all aspects. Build it across a specific timeline, describing exactly when you want certain actions to be accomplished and results obtained.

Use your journal to record your intentions—what your accomplishments will be, how they will be executed, and when they will be achieved. As you reach milestones, ensure you record (and reward) them.

> Don't make excuses for where you are in your life. Instead, set goals with a clear vision of where you intend to be and take immediate action to bring you to that defining point.

To move from a dream state into a life situation, you must begin the process of executing your plan. You must *actually* do something positive, which will move the idea from a simple thought process into the realm of real life.

We all dream; that's undeniable. It can be a wonderfully uplifting process of escapism and give us the strength to carry on when we feel overwhelmed. It's also a very real and functional practice enabling us to create an ideal life.

Dreams take absolutely no effort, while their effects on our futures can be literally life-altering.

> Your imagination is an immeasurably fertile garden for the foundations of human excellence. Once you learn to vividly imagine success and abundance, you have begun to sow the seeds of greatness in the garden of your life.

To have whatever you want in life, you must first decide exactly what it is you believe would make you happy and your life easier (aided by your dreams and visualization). Next you begin to formulate that clear, strong, and supported plan of action and put it into play to move the idea into reality.

Develop a mental picture of your ideal world. However, to truly realize that specific situation you've envisaged, you must take action. This does take effort—sometimes a great deal.

You could have the greatest plan ever devised. You may also have the most phenomenal product or service and/or the idea to accompany it. However, if you do nothing about it—if you fail to take positive action—then nothing will ever happen. The idea will remain in the dream realm. It's as simple as that.

> In every aspect of your life, you must learn to automatically throw open the doorway to opportunity. Align your thoughts, words, actions, and emotions and in this state allow the color, clarity, and depth of unfathomable possibilities to take shape.

In addition to your plan, also ensure you are totally aligned with what it is you're trying to attract—whether that's money, a new job, a house, a holiday, or a partner. It doesn't matter what it is, because once you are able to align yourself with your desires, you hold in your hand the keys to incredible riches.

When you are in alignment with your desires, you have at your fingertips the ability to release the power of your inner self. You immediately begin to diminish the hold of self-limiting beliefs and allow your positive thinking to create the ideal life.

The power of alignment in your life puts in your hands the real ability to create whatever it is you desire—whether that's happiness and true contentment, abundance, or more money. It reprograms your subconscious so that you can more easily believe in your own worthiness. This, in turn, triggers your ability to get up and go for what you want thereby attracting the ideal life, which can take you to some extraordinary places.

> If we only ever accept what's within our reach, we will never have the vision, drive, and commitment to search for and appreciate those wonderful opportunities which are just out of our grasp.

To be in total harmony, all aspects of your life and your desires must be in step. Your thoughts, words, and actions are in sync as you give power and direction to your life path. Remove the negatives as you become certain of your journey and support it explicitly.

At the end of the day, when you have time to reflect, consider what might be as opposed to what is. If you sit on your hands and fail to put your plan into action, absolutely nothing will change and ordinary will become the most extraordinary and abundant norm in your life.

> If you do nothing, then nothing will happen. However, everything can happen if you do something.

A plan of action can take almost any form. It's simply a blueprint on which to design your future, to put it on track and in the right direction—constantly forward. It's a positive action to begin your journey toward something better—something special. It should outline everything you want to do, the time in which you want to complete certain tasks, what your envisaged outcomes will be, and where you see yourself along a specific timeline.

Whether you want to invest in the stock market, buy property, create something special through your creative skills, begin a business, learn a trade, or return to studies, they all require a plan to come to life and take you in the direction you wish to go.

Outline the resources—time, materials, finances, and assistance—you'll need to accomplish this plan, the action required, and just who you should have in your corner helping you and on whom you can call from time to time for assistance and advice.

Include an evaluation process which will give you the ability to constantly appraise your plan to ensure you're heading in a forward direction.

Once I determine that failure is not an option, I've already succeeded.

Adopt a strict daily discipline. It's not enough to begin something by putting a plan into action and hoping it will have the momentum to continue. That's just the beginning of the plan/action process. You now have to be dedicated, focused, and ordered in your application. Stick to the plan and adopt rigorous processes according to any changing circumstances. This will see you continue on the path, even when times get a little tough.

When done correctly, daily disciplines will become weekly, monthly, and yearly as you begin to understand your business and pour your energy and determination into it. When you see it taking shape, your enthusiasm will kick in and carry you along.

Remember to reward yourself for great effort and achievement. It need not be big, only commensurate with your feat. You have the right to celebrate accomplishments as they occur. It will serve to reinforce your commitment to the journey, lift the spirits, and help drive the plan higher and further.

Success never hides. However, it remains elusive until commitment, drive, compassion, and gratitude become vital components in your everyday life plan.

Don't be afraid to dream big as you fill your plan with warmth and color. You can't take a journey if you have no idea where you want to go. You never set out on a holiday without preparation. Your plan of action is an itinerary of your intended expedition. It's always subject to change, but lays an initial guide track of where you're heading and all you will need to achieve the desired result.

The habits of truly successful people—the thinkers and doers throughout history—show that almost without exception the first (and most important) tool they adopt in their arsenal of success weapons is the ubiquitous plan of action. It's the crucial first step on the ladder to success. Without it, your dreams will flounder because they have no impetus or direction.

When you have specific goals, focus, drive, and a clear plan of action, opportunity will be attracted to your door like a magnet.

I'm drawn to two great quotes which are indicative of the drive and vision of those who have gone before us. The first is by Victor Hugo, French dramatist, novelist, and poet: "He who every morning plans the transaction of the day and follows out that plan, carries a thread that will guide him through the maze of the most busy life. But where no plan is laid, where the disposal of time is surrendered merely to the chance of incidence, chaos will soon reign."[6]

The second is by the amazing Napoleon Hill: "Create a definite plan for carrying out your desire and begin at once, whether you are ready or not, to put this plan into action."[7]

Both are very powerful and emotionally resonant truisms, pronouncing the fundamental need to formulate and enact a solid plan of action in your life.

> Looking at life through rose colored glasses is like living life in a bubble. You can never touch and feel the reality and passion of success after challenge.

First and foremost, resolve to enjoy the mission ahead. Try to avoid viewing it as a task. It's certainly not something to dislike, which is so often the case when we are in jobs which fail to excite us, but which we endure for a specific purpose (keeping a roof over our heads, clothes on our backs, and food on the table).

If you are prepared to tolerate the hard work for a better way of life, you have truly begun the process of attracting success into your world. You have to carry the right attitude with you.

Begin a venture which drives your passion and creativity. Find a niche market which truly interests you and something at which you know you can excel. While laboring under the weight of a mundane job, you might begin your project/s while having a steady income (even if initially on a part time basis).

> When your positive and focused belief patterns are stronger than the negative influences which bombard you every day, success and abundance will be your rewards.

If you're not yet an expert or you want additional information on your idea or vision, begin searching the Internet, asking people, and reading and viewing supporting material. Study the competition and the trends and get a good grasp of the market into which you intend to venture.

Irrespective of the kind of project you wish to commence, be driven by the thought of working at it each day. No matter what you choose, you need to understand that to give the undertaking any degree of longevity and the possibility of making money you must put energy, enthusiasm, and passion into your approach.

Always look forward with optimism and never worry about previous adverse events. Learn lessons from the challenges faced or run the risk of repeating them.

Once you stop living for yesterday, you begin the process of creating your ideal tomorrow. Today is simply a stopover on that journey to unimaginable personal success.

Create a brand which is uniquely you. Look at some of the countless thousands of successful businesses currently operating: Virgin, Trump, Microsoft, Facebook, Nike, Google, Starbucks, Gucci, the Kardashians, Calvin Klein, Mambo, Netscape, AOL, Versace, David Beckham, Qantas, Polo Ralph Lauren, Billabong, Ripcurl, Tommy Hilfiger, and Apple, to name just a few.

These companies (and individual creators) realized the critical importance of branding in the overall process of developing and maintaining a specific vision in the eyes (and minds) of consumers. They set about creating something special and memorable.

Consider how your business touches current and prospective customers/clients through advertising, PR, customer service, sales, marketing, and merchandising. These fundamental aspects must mesh seamlessly with one another for a new and in some cases reinvigorated brand to break through as a true contender and possible market leader.

Be proud of who you are and what you do. Stand by yourself and your product, and always act with integrity, compassion, and faith.

Your plan should present you as you are (and as you would like others to perceive you). The more real you appear to the public—whether as a speaker, entrepreneur, or in whatever light you wish others to perceive you or your brand—the greater will be the possibility that others will remember you in that light, as the real and successful person you are. This should be a tangible and ongoing component of your plan. Use it as a powerful motivator.

Never present yourself or your business as anything other than the reality of what you have. Customers will see through the ruse and you will fail. It will be almost impossible to resurrect a company/brand/personality from the ashes when the public turns its back on you due to untruthful representation. To maintain longevity, your integrity must remain intact.

> It doesn't matter where you are in this moment, because with the right dreams and actions the next seconds, minutes, days, and weeks can mark the beginning of a whole new and exciting journey of personal discovery and success.

Constantly review your plan to ensure you're on track. Things can change in your day-to-day life, which can impact your view of the future and the development of your plan. It pays to take a step back occasionally and have an objective view of your progress. It can be difficult to remain permanently engaged. Give yourself a short break from the constant and consistent action.

It's *your* plan, *your* dreams and visions, and above all *your* life. Therefore, and although it is a blueprint for *your* future, try and occasionally look at it from a detached point of view and be honest in *your* assessment of *your* plan and *your* chosen direction. If necessary, get that all-important outside advice and assistance for an objective point of view. It could prove to be the critical aspect of *your* longevity.

Outcomes are also a fundamental component of that plan. There are in fact two types—*desired* and *probable*—and they depend heavily upon the action you take. When your plan is meticulously constructed and results-driven and your actions positive, focused, and determined, your emotions should also be congruent with your actions. It's now the probable and desired outcomes can ideally be in harmony.

The outcomes should be viewed as a yardstick against which you can quantify your action and truly understand the nature of the path you're traveling. Ensure both desired and probable outcomes are in complete synchronization with those aspects of your life which bring you love, happiness, recognition, courage, drive, commitment, and gratitude.

When you choose to be happy and more optimistic, you refuse to accept negativity in your life. Continue to fuel your dreams of success with drive, passion, determination, and a positive plan of action in spite of the obstacles you face. You cannot avoid success and abundance.

Refrain from indirectly sabotaging your efforts with irrational and/or irresponsible behavior. Conscious effort, ongoing determination, and inspiration are all necessary to achieve the success which will ultimately come your way. Approach all tasks associated with your plan with positive thoughts and actions.

You've probably heard the term *massive action*. In terms of your business it's an oxymoron, because there should be no difference between *action* and *massive action* in terms of the serious steps needed to achieve success and abundance in life.

If you are driven to succeed and you have your plan in place, then it makes perfect sense that any action you take to advance your project will be massive to bring about the desired result in the shortest amount of time. Anything else would be a compromise. You owe it to yourself and your plan to give 100 percent effort and focus to what you want to achieve to bring about the ideal life.

By now you've no doubt begun to understand the fundamental necessity for a plan—a direction that will take you from where you are, feeling as if you're walking on a treadmill, to where you want to be. That special, real, and tangible place where you can realize your vision of a great future—something concrete, over and above the dream of a better life. You should now understand the meaning of attracting wonderful things into your life with newfound drive and enthusiasm, which is constantly evolving within you.

You were born to win; that's an indisputable fact. Once you truly believe that, understand it, and expect it, success and abundance will be within reach.

There are several undeniable facts in life. We're all born, we live, and eventually we die. There's not a lot we can do about the probability of the first or the inevitability of the last. It is, however, the intermediate which opens a whole world of possibilities to each of us, but in different ways. My wants and needs will undoubtedly be quite different from yours. What you receive from your life and the efforts you put in depend largely upon those wants and needs and the steps you take to achieve that end.

Every successful entrepreneur ensures their ventures have sound and supported plans of action around which their visions of success and abundance are clearly defined and developed. Your plan will allow you to navigate toward your dreams. It paves the way for a sound foundation and projection of how and across what time frame your future will evolve, the type of service you intend to provide, and what your desired (and probable) outcomes (and income) will be.

Once you decide on the type of business you want and direction you wish to go, next set about taking the crucial steps to ensure the venture goes where you want it to—through your clear and unambiguous plan.

Be sure of every step you take in life because each forms an integral part of the journey to your ultimate destiny.

The ensuing action you take should be designed to further your plan and begin to deliver the life you want. Maintain the right frame of mind as each day comes and goes and your plan begins to unfold. Feel the excitement (and the nerves) mount as you edge ever closer to your dream.

Always make time for leisure activities. Balance your life and avoid the possibility of your batteries running low so you remain upbeat and focused. It will help you to remain focused on your current path. Everyone is entitled to a reward, especially for hard work that achieves goals. Take time out from your tasks and enjoy the fruits of your labor. You've earned it, so take the time to stop, rest, recuperate, and celebrate.

Conversely, when you encounter problems stop, think, and act. Look at the obstacle from all sides and, if necessary, seek assistance and advice from those who have the prerequisite knowledge and experience and are best placed to answer your questions and give you the advice you require.

If you have a mentor/coach, seek the appropriate advice. If you don't have one, try and enlist the help of a successful person with whom you can discuss the problem—someone who can work with you to put you back on the right track and keep you there.

Next time someone offers a kind word or helping hand and you know that person has a genuine interest in your life and possesses the experience to show you the way through the maze, accept the gesture with gratitude and allow yourself the freedom to feel the warmth and empowerment of friendship. It's then you'll know you've sown the initial seeds of success.

> When you open yourself to the genuine and selfless assistance from others, you also open yourself to endless guidance of those who have your best interests at heart.

This assistance might come in the form of a coach or an invitation to attend industry related seminars. You might buy some books, CDs, and DVDs to give you the momentum necessary to move you out of the rut and onto the crest of the hill where you can feel the sunshine on your face and see the way ahead more clearly. If you're truly passionate about your business and serious about your future, take the positive steps required to help realize your dream and prevent it from becoming derailed.

Any monetary outlay will be worthwhile if you put the information to use and begin to remove the blocks. It will have real value when you begin to once again move forward with a renewed enthusiasm and determination. Sometimes there are things which you simply can't handle on your own. That's the time to ask for support.

I strenuously discourage any individual from getting into financial difficulty at any time. Should this occur, I suggest professional assistance and advice be sought before it becomes a real problem. This counsel should come from a legally qualified and certified accountant and/or legal practitioner. Certainly from someone who has financial management experience.

> Never waste valuable time worrying about what might have been. Put that powerful plan into action, embrace your vision, and set sail with determination toward a celebration of what can be.

An integral component of your plan of action is to build around you a strong support base including friends, family, and where possible mentors/coaches. Family and friends are ideal for input and advice, moral support, love, and encouragement when the going gets a little tough. Mentors/coaches are necessary because they can remain objective in their approach and have the experience and knowledge to help you forge a path ahead.

Find one who can relate to you on both a personal and professional level and work with them to reignite your confidence and give you valuable information/advice. It will help you to find the commitment, determination, and focus to develop and support your strong plan of action. Build it on your individual dreams and visions, fired by your drive and energy. Never rely on others solely to develop your plan of action or live your life for you.

> Your selfless assistance to others is priceless. The positive energy found in the success you achieve leaves visible tracks for all eternity.

These leaders have adopted and often developed plausible strategies designed specifically to alleviate problems, explain pitfalls, and provide advice on navigating that often obscured path. This invaluable assistance will ease pressure and help you to reach your goals quicker and easier.

When offered the appropriate assistance and you see your life rapidly change and evolve into something quite extraordinary, you quickly learn the value found in following the pathways which have been forged by great leaders. Trusting their advice and assistance, which sees your life change in extraordinary ways, means you also trust your inner voice.

> Life is a wonderful journey of discovery. Make up your mind to take it as far as you can. Strap yourself in with confidence; open your eyes, your heart, and your mind; and ensure you invite your passion, persistence, and dreams along for the ride.

Don't rely solely on the assistance of those around you, because at the end of the day as the doors close and staff and friends return to their families, the longevity of your enterprise is still in your hands. Twenty-four hours a day, seven days a week you have responsibility for your business. Nurture it; respect it; build it: Give it longevity.

To commence your plan of action, envision the type of business venture or undertaking you want and which you believe will deliver the kind of life you desire for yourself and your cherished family. Harvey Mackay, the wonderful author and internationally recognized speaker, said, "Find something you love to do and you'll never have to work a day in your life."[8]

Though this sounds simplistic, you would never benefit from laboring at a job you detest. It makes sense to enjoy what you do, and if you don't, find something that lights your fire and is worth getting out of bed for every day. It means your thoughts and actions are in harmony with your values and therefore make for a more balanced life.

> Never be afraid of success. Be challenged by failure.

Base your decision on specific criteria according to needs, interests, and passions. Once you know and understand exactly what you want in your life and where you wish that energy, drive, and commitment to take you, begin to methodically build your plan.

It's imperative you understand the nature of what it is you desire. For instance, it's fruitless adopting a plan of action built around the ideal life, but which is set on a platform of something implausible or about which you know very little. It must be realistic and fire your passion and enthusiasm.

> When you come to believe that the sun shines in and on your life every day, you will know that although you may not always see and feel its warming rays, you'll find the determination to see it and appreciate where it shines.

Know your material, and if you have little idea about the subject/product but you know beyond question it is something you want to do and it truly drives you, set about finding out everything there is to know about it. Become an expert in the field and drive that passion and vision further than you ever thought possible.

Next, it's a really good idea to look at the competition. Find out how many other people are doing what you would like to do. See how they operate and simply do it better. Decide whether or not it would be viable and cost effective. Make your product/service/idea much more appealing than the opposition and your subject material more attractive—add color, vigor, depth, enthusiasm, and creativity to what you do. Give it your personal touch, be totally committed, and add 100 percent energy and passion to the business.

> Watching, waiting, and procrastinating will only detract from visualizing, creating, persisting, and succeeding.

Approach all commercial dealings with honesty, determination, and gratitude. Radiate warmth and compassion—it will become infectious and draw people in. If you approach any task with integrity and openness, you'll throw out the welcome mat for like-minded people to become a part of your abundant world.

A friendly approach acts like a flame on a dark night. You will of course attract those who might be less than desirable to the growth and development of your business or enterprise; that's human nature. On the whole, however, a friendly, honest, and compassionate approach will send the clear message to others that you are a person with whom they can confidently conduct business. You make others feel comfortable with and happy to be in your company.

To become a successful and high-level performer, decide what is most important for your future. Set out projections of just where you see yourself and your enterprise positioned in three months, six months, one year, and even five and ten years. This is important to determine where you want to be according to the effort you put into your plans. Constantly reevaluate your position to try to avoid disenchantment creeping into your life.

> Step outside your comfort zone at least once in your life. If you leave doubt and fear behind, the view becomes extraordinary and life-changing.

Achievement in any business venture depends on a strong platform. Start with an idea which fires your passion and where you have sound knowledge and expertise. Once you've done that, begin identifying (potential) problems and instigate programs designed to successfully deal with those issues. This will help to develop your business acumen.

There's always a great deal of work to be done along the journey to creating and maintaining a sound commercial enterprise. Once you've instigated suitable programs to cover most contingencies, you may now face the often daunting task of convincing others you are the right person with the appropriate tools and skills to solve their problem and fulfil their need. On occasion, instances will arise for which you have no plan. Deal with them as they occur. Stop and think objectively.

Although of importance to any business, this aspect can be quite challenging because while you may have the tools, skills, and experience, if you are unable to convince others of your ability, the door will remain shut and the phone silent. Your business will eventually fold. That's a sad reality of life.

> When you have faith in yourself and your ability, you will find the courage to step down with pride and confidence from the safe arms of giants rather than wither in their shadows.

Prioritize your goals and put effort into the one you feel is the most important. Select the most central task; it should become the one on which you focus your energy and drive, while not totally disregarding the others. See it through to completion and feel the wave of confidence and warmth pass over you as you begin to move to the next task in your overall plan for success.

When you are focused on success and are dedicated to building a business, the drive and commitment will spill over into all areas of your life. Your various projects will mesh in so many ways, as you utilize the same tenacity and systematically build the future you want through the projects you undertake.

> When you are truly happy and content with your life and smile at the world, you radiate warmth and, like a beacon, draw others to you.

Write down your ideas, plans, and goals no matter how crazy or strange they seem. Refer to them often so you won't forget them and become disengaged from the real reasons you began the journey. Refer to them when uncertainty calls to bring yourself back in line with your ideal life.

Each of us has suffered degrees of doubt at times in our lives. It generally hits when we're feeling low. Uncertainty grows from many areas, such as a perceived lack of action in our lives, negativity from others which creeps into our psyche, diminished self-belief and feelings of self-worth, illness, injury, and often just because we allow it to get inside our heads.

Have a clear and unconstrained picture in your mind's eye of just where you will be in those set timeframes (three months, six months, etc.). Support your projections in your journal with the necessary lists of the positive aspects about your undertaking. Fill it with uplifting and inspirational information. Make sure however, your projections aren't too ambitious or implausible; this might cause you some angst when you fail to achieve them.

> Once you decide beyond all doubt that success is your one true goal, opportunity will begin to present itself according to your most prized values.

Reduce those feelings of dejection which creep up on you from time to time by remaining positive, focused, and determined. If you give them power in your life, they can become quite damaging to your drive and perceptions of self-worth.

There are many ways to eliminate doubt from your life and keep yourself on track for success. In spite of what might impact you, occasionally step back and take a breath. Even take a momentary break from the fast lane. This brief action will assist you to keep focused and determined and recharge your batteries.

Keep the cold fingers of uncertainty at bay through positive and committed thoughts. When they creep in, seek the assistance of your mentor or coach to keep you emotionally buoyant and provide an objective view on your situation. Continue your realistic projections and don't become disillusioned through making them too ambitious or unrealistic.

An action plan is imperative because it sets up *your* direction and gives *you* the fuel necessary to push forward with *your* vision to achieve a variety of positive outcomes specific to *your* dreams.

> When you learn to become totally secure within yourself and are truly proud of who you are and the journey you're traveling, you develop the capacity to resist the insecurities of others and deny them the ability to negatively impact your life.

It's important to remember this is not a business or marketing plan. It's a map—an overall view of your life and direction, which you create and maintain to keep you focused and aligned with your dreams and visions according to your needs and wants.

A business plan is a more inclusive document outlining all aspects of your proposed business venture. It includes important topics like the executive summary (objectives, costs/revenue summaries, any assumptions/aspects unique to your business); company description (overview, governance, location, image, etc.); product/service (what you offer, pricing models, delivery mechanisms, customer service, etc.); market (target and why, current state, future/expansion); risks (possible/probable vulnerabilities, any negative impacts); competitors (present/future); operational plan (infrastructure, personnel, product selection/delivery processes, accounting practices, auditing, customer management); sales/marketing outline (reaching the target market and generating revenue); financial plan (establishment/ongoing/expansion, costs and projections); and an exit strategy (what your future plans might be).

Hold on to your dream with confidence and passion and strive for your goals with every fiber of your being. Know beyond question you're on the right path, even when aspects of your life threaten to engulf you and those dark clouds of uncertainty gather. Stay focused and driven and remind yourself just why you are doing what you are.

Always ensure your dreams have a true purpose. They must create a pathway to something better and more outstanding than you have now. Give them color and direction. Give them heart. Give them life.

Your journal/diary is an ideal avenue through which to outline your action plan and use as a ready reference when you stray from your path. The more positive and descriptive you make it, the more supportive it will become.

Celebrate every success; each serves to close the gaps in your journey. By being positive, determined, and driven and sticking to your plan with enthusiasm and purpose, you're consistently building on your success platform and giving yourself permission to move forward with passion and purpose toward your goals. As each passes, quietly celebrate the milestone and move to the next with enthusiasm.

You can reflect on life past, but don't spend too much time in that realm; you run the risk of dwelling unduly on historic mishaps, obstacles, and problems. I always suggest to my clients they briefly look at where they've come from and enjoy the past accomplishments (not fret over the disappointments) before moving enthusiastically forward to the wonderful new destination.

Feel proud of where you are in this very moment, in spite of any obstacles you've faced and setbacks you may have encountered. It's your focus, determination, and self-belief which are important drivers. Be confident of the steps you've completed to get to this special place, the many goals you've achieved, and the direction your life is taking you at this very time.

> Don't waste time lost in the darkness of the past. Use your drive, focus, and enthusiasm to create an abundantly bright and vivid vision of the future you want and immerse yourself.

Believe beyond all else that your plan and all it encompasses is truly carrying you toward the (perhaps once elusive) light at the end of the tunnel. It's a wonderful and abundant destination created by you; it holds your dreams for a more fulfilled life. Believe it, begin to see your future unfold, and start to embrace the journey.

While waiting for your plan to take root and flower, you'll need an income derived from some form of work which you may not necessarily like. When you have money coming in, it releases the stress and enables you to focus on your plan and build upon your dream. It bolsters your confidence and aids in keeping your feelings of self-worth buoyant.

Have unwavering faith in your plan and fully embrace change according to the opportunities which arise along the way. Give yourself permission to be happy and always keep the horizon in sight.

NOTES

1. John L. Beckley, http://rainmakermarketingandsales.wordpress.com/2012/11/14/most-people-dont-plan-to-fail-they-fail-to-plan-john-l-beckley/.

2. SBA, "Frequently Asked Questions about Small Business," SBA Office of Advocacy, September 2012, 3, http://www.sba.gov/sites/default/files/FAQ_Sept_2012.pdf.

3. Bruce Lee, "The Path to Truth and Success," The Bruce Lee Foundation, accessed June 13, 2014, http://www.bruceleefoundation.com/index.cfm/page/THE-WISDOM-OF-BRUCE-LEE-This-Issue%3A-%25E2%2580%259CThe-Path-to-Truth-and-Success%25E2%2580%259D/cdid/10661/pid/10225.

4. Henry Ford, *My Life and Work: An Autobiography of Henry Ford* (CreateSpace Independent Publishing Platform, 2013), 18.

5. Mark Twain, http://www.searchquotes.com/quotation/There_are_a_thousand_excuses_for_failure,_but_never_a_good_reason./510418/.

6. Victor Hugo, http://www.quotationspage.com/quote/2785.html.

7. Napoleon Hill, http://thinkexist.com/quotation/create_a_definite_plan_for_carrying_out_your/324443.html.

8. Harvey MacKay, https://www.goodreads.com/quotes/430570-find-something-you-love-to-do-and-you-ll-never-work.

When life gets a little tough and you feel like letting go
and giving up, remember it's often when you put your
life into extra time that you can find the strength and
clarity to rise above adversity and realize your dreams.

LESSONS LEARNED

1. A supported plan of action is a crucial step for success.

2. Problems can infiltrate all aspects of life if you allow them to.

3. Be disciplined, set time frames, and seek assistance/support.

4. Record ideas/goals in your diary no matter how impossible they seem.

5. Review your plan; ensure it's in harmony with your values.

6. Success is measured by outcomes—desired and probable—depending upon your actions.

7. Don't allow thoughtless/irrational behavior to indirectly sabotage success.

8. Remain accountable for your actions and take responsibility for everything you do.

9. Replace bad habits with good through reinforcement and repetition.

10. Take time to reflect and have gratitude for your great life.

11. Accept a kind word and helping hand with gratitude.

12. If you're determined and focused, any action is "massive."

13. Make your product/service better than the opposition.

14. Build a strong support base and a positive state of mind.

15. Never rely solely on others. Forge your own path to success.

16. Appreciate quality assistance and understand that success leaves tracks for all eternity.

17. Build your plan of action around what you want.

18. Reward yourself for completed tasks and achievements.

19. Believe in yourself and have courage no matter what occurs.

20. Give yourself permission to be happy and successful.

21. Always keep the horizon in view.

Chapter 10

SALES AND MARKETING KNOWLEDGE

It is never what happens in our lives that has the most impact on us. Instead, it's the choices we make in our decisions to deal with those occurrences that will determine the caliber of person we ultimately become and the measure of the success we enjoy.

As a business owner, you'll be involved, to varying degrees, in the sales and marketing aspects of your enterprise which will require effort to keep it on track. You have to constantly market your business/product/service to ensure it reaches the largest possible audience and continues optimum sales.

If you have the money to pay a sales and marketing guru, then more power to you. However, most small businesses are starved of initial start-up capital and require a great deal of effort and input from the owner just to stay afloat.

When you embark on a new plan of action, brimming with enthusiasm and fired by your new and exciting ideas, you have to know where you're going, what you're doing, and how to present yourself to the market in the best possible light.

In everything I do I give my very best and focus totally on what I want to achieve. This ensures the outcomes will exceed my expectations.

It makes no sense to be passionate about a fantastic plan only to see it fall in a heap because you have no marketing or sales experience/knowledge. You don't have to be a professional, but it's imperative you have at least a basic knowledge of what it takes to get your program off the ground and keep it powering along.

A rudimentary understanding of sales and marketing can be obtained through various private and government programs. There is always a number of high powered seminars taking place at any one time, and it's important you find one with values that are in harmony with your own. Once you understand the power of knowledge, invest fully in yourself to ensure you give your business/idea the best possible chance of success.

> To be successful in life, appreciate and instigate all the necessary skills to push your business to the stars.

These programs are generally not free, although there are often introductory evenings through which you can gain some great information and a good feel for both the presenter and the material.

There are also many short but intensive courses and seminars which can provide the initial tools, depending upon your chosen path. Once you gain the necessary experience, you may wish to advance further with your studies. Find something which resonates with you and your ideals, lock it in, and enjoy the ride.

This will give you the confidence to step from your comfort zone and embrace additional skills with the capacity to see your plan gather strength and momentum. Without the power of sales and marketing, you run the risk of failure—not because the idea was wrong or poor, but because you didn't possess the necessary skills and knowledge to give it the momentum necessary to bring it to life and show it to the world.

It doesn't matter how good your business/product/service might be. If no one knows about it—if you have no solid sales or marketing strategy in place—your product/service will continue to gather dust.

> Once you become highly motivated and successful, you become an
> inspiration to yourself and others and lose the inclination to be dependent.

If you're not initially in a position to spend money on your business, at least begin with a comprehensive website. That's the first tool you should create. It can be built for a few dollars, and through various sites, such as Wix and Wordpress, you rent a domain name and start the creation process. Alternatively, you can pay someone to create and manage the site for you.

Once the website is up and running, obtain membership to the many social/business networking sites available. The sites include Facebook, LinkedIn, Twitter, Plaxo, Instagram, Maven, and many others. They hold literally millions of prospective customers and a cache of help and assistance. You can begin the process of publicizing yourself and your business, building a network of support, and attracting the clients and customers you need.

In addition to network memberships, it's also a great idea to begin posting blogs. They're really easy to set up through various sites such as Wordpress, Blogger, Tumblr, and Posterous. There are also some great sites which help you set up your blog and get started. You can also post brief videos on YouTube, LinkedIn and Facebook to continue the networking process. YouTube is also a great resource for the important topics of networking, marketing and sales.

Once you're set up and are familiar with all your networking tools, use them to direct clients and contacts to your regular products and services. Develop a mailing list through using opt-in links on your web page and your regular visitors to the blogs. Keep them updated with interesting information about you and your business and any product/service/material advice and information. This will inevitably elevate your profile with the very real capacity to present you in a positive light as an expert in your chosen field.

Once these strategies are in place and you begin to move forward with a degree of confidence on your overall plan of action, customers will be attracted and business will begin to grow.

A firm belief in your idea/business gives you the courage and focus to get out and do what's necessary to move forward with passion and purpose. Success doesn't just happen; it requires a great deal of hard work. The responsibility is yours to do the best you can with your life and future.

Ensure you're armed with all the skills and knowledge necessary to realize the success you want (and deserve). The positive and results-driven actions you take will help ensure that your *desired* and *probable* outcomes are in unison.

Give your idea the best possible chance of success by believing in yourself and your dreams, working with purpose and dedication, and knowing beyond question that you deserve remarkable success in your life. You must take all the positive steps necessary to bring your idea to life and realize all you are capable of achieving.

> I know beyond question that the future is not based on the present, which is all I see before me. I have the power and courage to change everything so that my future is more remarkable than I can possibly imagine.

It's not necessary to attend university/college to obtain enough knowledge to arm yourself with the requisite skills to find and embrace success, though for many it represents part of their desired journey to fulfilment. Those who wish to pursue tertiary qualifications should be encouraged to do so and supported every step of the way.

I advise any business owner to gain the appropriate knowledge to move forward with confidence and quiet assurance. If you want to attend a small business course or enroll in tertiary studies in a business discipline, then do it. In addition to boosting your confidence, you'll need every ounce of knowledge when you decide to jump into the mix with your new business venture.

You can't afford to take unnecessary risks with your future. There are specific sales and marketing skills which will assist you to advance on your goals. Once you make up your mind to be successful, gaining this knowledge should be paramount in your plan.

> When you live your life according to the strong and unerring belief that failure is impossible, fear of disappointment is reduced and every action is calculated to succeed.

It's not enough to simply want to do something positive and fulfilling with your life. Once you dream of that better and more empowered existence, you need to take the required action and follow through for the long haul with passion and persistence to give your plan the best possible outcomes.

Ensure your efforts and enthusiasm are in total unison. That means doing more than simply hoping everything will turn out and crossing your fingers. Do what's necessary to protect your business, product, and/or enterprise, giving it the best possible chance of success.

The secret to your business success and the enrichment of your future is ultimately in your hands. The decisions you make and actions you take will decide the direction your future will take.

Calculated steps—big and small—will assist your forward momentum. Stop when necessary to assess your progress, but remain connected to your passion and determination and the reasons why you initially began your amazing journey.

No matter who you are, where you're from, or what has impacted your life, how you feel about yourself and the vision and determination you have to succeed are the driving forces which will decide the degree of success and abundance you enjoy.

LESSONS LEARNED

1. When you own your own business, you are involved in sales and marketing.

2. In any new business venture, you have to know how to present yourself professionally.

3. You should give yourself the benefit of basic sales and marketing knowledge.

4. Every business must have a sales and marketing strategy.

5. Belief in your business will give you the courage and confidence to move it forward.

6. Private and government programs provide basic sales and marketing information.

7. Ensure the desired and probable outcomes are in unison.

8. Gain the necessary knowledge to move your business/idea forward with confidence.

9. Consider the various social networking sites and blog postings to elevate your profile.

10. Action and persistence will give your business the best possible chance of success.

11. Continue to do the best you can with your life and future.

Chapter 11

EFFECTIVE COMMUNICATION

Where you go, what you do, how you communicate, what
you think, and the way you look at the world will have
a resounding impact on your future and success.

Communication in some form and on some level is paramount in all aspects of our daily lives. We constantly interact with each other, whether at home, with friends and neighbors, on the street with strangers, on the bus, at the shops, in taxis, at the office, in a restaurant or at a sporting event. We communicate every day of our lives. We need that valuable interaction to maintain a reasonable standard of living.

A good communicator is a good listener and generally comfortable with who they are and confident in their own personal space. They give the other person room to enter into open dialogue across a range of topics with the freedom to express a point of view.

Effective communication is a fundamental step to empowering ourselves and our lives.

To be an effective communicator, learn to listen—with your head and heart. It's not always the spoken word which provides the clearest message.

Non-verbal cues are crucial to interpersonal interaction. They lead us to further understand the real art of communication as we begin building those strong relationships.

Effective conversation flows easily. There are no flat spots nor is there hesitation. Interest is generally shown on both sides of this process to allow it to move confidently.

Learn to really listen to what another has to say (this is a true skill in itself and can take some time to master) and you'll have commenced the process of meaningful conversation.

Ask open-ended questions, which require more than a simple *yes* or *no* answer. This encourages and empowers the other person to thoughtfully express and share a pertinent viewpoint.

You must be on top of your game at all times and seek to reflect your personality and character in your communication. This is more effective in open forum presentation than the written word, though this too is important and should also reflect your character (to a point)—but in line with what's being sought.

> When you communicate effectively, you transmit to others the true nature of your character and personality and allow the real you to shine through.

Good communication encompasses the ability to tune in to what's going on around you at all times, in all aspects of your life. When you take the time to make the connection and truly listen to the messages being exchanged, you'll begin to understand the nature of effective communication.

This means developing the capacity to get your message to another person in a way that can be clearly understood. Language is not always a barrier to this interaction when you are able to communicate on a passionate level. This can happen on many planes in both personal and business relationships.

There will be occasions however, when you are required to remove the emotion from your communication. In these instances you should stick to the facts and relay a situation as it is, rather than as you perceive it (or would like it) to be. This can be difficult but is paramount if you are to move forward to a resolution.

It's also important in effective communication to show empathy, which is an indication of your respect for the beliefs and opinions of the other person (people). Be flexible, willing to communicate, and always accept that compromise might be necessary to achieve a positive result.

> To be an effective communicator, you must also learn the tactful art of compromise. To meet another halfway displays power, vision, and courage. It also breaks down barriers and assists in building friendships.

The success of that interaction relies on a number of prime factors. First, you need to understand the nature of and reason for the communication. Perhaps it's simply a friendly exchange with others regarding any number of things, such as a great football game on the weekend, the hockey or baseball scores or the swimming races our children entered at school. Perhaps it's more in-depth issues such as politics, business or religion. Maybe it's a heart to heart talk with someone about relationships, the scourge of illicit drugs or some injury/illness to a family member or friend. It could be a formal presentation on science, medicine, sales, marketing, construction, or any one of countless topics.

Once our mind comprehends the nature of and reason for the communication, we immediately know the level on which the interaction is to take place. We're therefore more able to react appropriately with balanced and thoughtful responses.

Effective communication is the ability to confidently express a particular viewpoint in the most succinct and focused way so as to better understand another's point of view. It allows for opinions to be shared and debated on any number of topics. This is imperative for both your personal and professional platforms.

As an effective communicator you can freely, confidently, and often passionately inform others of your view of life, what you expect from a specific set of circumstances, and how these can and do impact your world. You can also inform others when a situation impacts you negatively.

> Effective communication is your ability to understand the impact of your words and actions on others and the world around you.

As a speaker/presenter, there are three core (and inter-linked) components to the whole aspect of effective face-to-face presentations (communication):

- What you say (the spoken word) is 7 percent.
- The way you say it (elements of the voice) is 38 percent.
- The entire package forms an almost unbelievable 55 percent.

The way you dress, move, and fully engage others will determine the success or otherwise of your communication. Carry yourself with poise and dignity, power and passion, drive and commitment. Discover and nurture confidence in and respect for your own point of view and that expressed by another person.

Ensure you present well. Dress appropriately for the particular occasion and prepare adequately. The assessment process will begin before you even open your mouth, so the way you appear will make the first impression.

Prepare before a presentation—whether in a small office environment or with an audience of hundreds. This means knowing every aspect of your subject material and understanding your audience. It also means visualizing the audience listening and responding professionally to your performance.

It's also important to warm up your voice with various exercises to give it depth and resonance. All this preparation is referred to as "getting in the zone." *Proper preparation prevents a poor performance!*

If you lack vocal strength, it's a good idea to have professional training so you develop power and resonance in your voice. Adopt strategies which reduce pitch, inflection, intonation, and modulation problems. This can be attributed to nerves and a degree of uncertainty with either yourself or the subject material.

Build the confidence in all aspects of your performance so your voice becomes authoritative, with the resultant depth to your vocal range. This will elevate your presentations and give you far more credibility in the eyes of your audience.

Recommendations follow great presentations.

You will suffer nerves—even the most successful speakers have some degree of anxiety before any appearance. It gives you the edge and keeps you focused. It can also hinder your presentation, so ensure you prepare well to control your adrenaline levels so as not to inhibit your professional delivery.

In spite of the inner turmoil you may be experiencing, believe in yourself and your ability. Tell yourself you are a powerful and impressive speaker and presenter. Exude a calm but upbeat exterior to put your audience at ease and fill them with confidence and optimism.

Practice in front of workmates and family members to build your confidence and help to eliminate some problems in your presentation. You should also practice in front of the mirror so you can see firsthand how others will see you.

A formal presentation should make the audience a fundamental part of the interaction. Use eye contact and personalize your delivery. Make individuals feel a part of the entire process. Draw them in and keep them interested. The content of your speech and your ability to engage must compel your audience to listen and subsequently connect with you.

This is also important when giving a presentation to a camera. The lens becomes your audience. Don't be deterred by the fact that the greater audience could number in the tens of thousands and even more. You might even personalize the lens by visualizing a face on it of someone you are comfortable with. This technique can relax you and assist in bringing depth and warmth to your presentation.

Turn your presentations into individual conversations with each audience member. The focus must be on the audience rather than you as the speaker. Irrespective of the material you're presenting, use stories to add color and depth; draw your audience in; make your connection complete and compelling. Avoid self-aggrandizement; simply tell a story which supports the journey on which you take your audience.

Once you understand the energy and mood in the room, tailor your presentation accordingly. Put the audience at ease so they can more readily absorb the details.

Ensure the information you impart is decipherable and digestible without overloading the audience. Communicate on an appropriate level to ensure you can be understood. Avoid being condescending at all costs.

> When you open your mind and your heart, you allow others to see and understand who you are and what you stand for.

An audience comes to your presentation to interact—to listen and take away with them all the information necessary to spur them to take action in one or more areas of life. You must be engaging, interesting, and at times funny (where appropriate) to connect with your audience; relax, and empower them. Connect with them through your own energy, passion and determination.

You are a mentor and teacher for those moments you're on stage. You have information to impart to the audience, so never disappoint by being under prepared. Know your subject material and deliver it in a sharp, crisp, concise, and compelling manner.

In building a public speaking platform, understand the fundamental nature of communication. People will want to listen to you and clients will wish to learn from you if you can hold their attention and they can relate to the subject material. An audience needs to feel empowered and enlightened. They need to learn something from your presentation and take away some gems.

> Your life is like a wonderful oil painting comprised of countless colors, emotions, hues, shades, and brush strokes. Each adds to the nature and value of the painting, working together to complete a true masterpiece.

No matter what line of business you're engaged in, you'll need to be an effective and inspiring communicator. Your customers/clients will need a thorough understanding of exactly what you do, the nature of your product/services/business, and be able to walk away with a clear understanding of your visions and ideals. Your longevity will hinge on this.

The workplace will never function professionally without open channels of communication. This means a free and unimpeded flow of knowledge, ideas, and suggestions to and from management and among peers. It helps to eliminate ambiguity, misunderstanding, and misinformation.

Effective and appropriate communication should always be encouraged. It breaks down barriers and gives employees a real sense of purpose. It empowers them to work diligently toward common goals and sanctions them to add value and depth to the organization without fear of reprisal through misunderstanding.

A business, like a clock, requires all parts working in harmony. Without one key element, the operation can't function as it should. When all components are working together, aided by effective communication, the business will begin to evolve.

> As you open your mouth to communicate, ensure what you have to say is interesting, productive, and supported. Always ensure your heart and mind are also open.

Even in difficult times, it's important all employees are kept informed on matters relating to progress. This enables educated decisions to be made ensuring, as far as possible, that critical information is not misunderstood or misinterpreted. There are, of course, times when information will not and cannot be forthcoming from management in relation to programs, deals, and impacting decisions regarding specific fiscal and administration matters.

It's important, however, that employees are not left out of the loop altogether. Give them information relevant to their positions to reduce the possibility of damaging rumors and unnecessary concerns regarding employment security. Without care and consideration, problems can become wildly exaggerated, requiring damage control.

Open and effective communication channels allay fears and prevent unsupported conclusions being reached based on half-truths and idle, "back office" gossip. It also limits misinterpretation and innuendo. It heads off issues before they become problems for the workplace

> Your destiny never evolves as the result of one isolated action. It's always the culmination of all life's individual performances, words, thoughts, and feelings. These determine your success or otherwise.

Written communication also requires due care and attention. If your writing is flat, dull, and boring, you won't keep your audience/business contacts connected to you for long. Use colorful and descriptive words and add humor (where appropriate and depending upon the nature of the communication).

Engage the reader by making your written material interesting and relevant. Every piece of correspondence is intended to tell a story, no matter how brief. Spelling and grammar should be as accurate as possible. If in doubt, buy a thesaurus or have another person (with good spelling and grammatical skills) proofread the document for you. Never rely on your computer spell check—that's one road to certain disaster.

If you're feeling angry or aggrieved, make sure you're in a more positive frame of mind before you "put pen to paper." Once something is written and dispatched, it can't be retrieved or retracted. It has the capacity to negatively impact you and your business. The lesson is—think before you do or say anything so regret doesn't become a constant in your future.

Leave nothing to chance, because first impressions leave lasting imprints and are fundamental to the longevity of your business.

Strength and longevity in personal relationships also rely heavily on communication. Let a partner, spouse, sibling, child, or close friend know how you're feeling and what your reactions might be at a particular time and in response to a specific word/action/emotion.

Without effective communication, there would be no efficient means for individuals to rationally discuss matters. This could lead to issues being bottled up; they can fester and possibly lead to a person reaching boiling point, resulting in a response or reaction totally out of proportion to the initial trigger. This generally proves damaging to every person involved in that situation.

When we allow problems to fester unchecked, we are adversely impacting our health. This unfortunately creates a whole new set of problems for an individual to deal with (see Chapter 8: "Taking Care of Your Health and Fitness").

Successful communication is neither a secret nor a coveted ritual. It's a fundamental tool for successful relationship building. Embrace it and soar.

I have no doubt each of us has at one time or another reacted adversely to a particular catalyst in either a business or personal situation when, had we openly communicated our feelings in the first instance—verbalizing our fears, doubts, worries, uncertainties, or concerns—we may have averted a boil over and subsequent knee-jerk reaction.

It's paramount you learn to converse in all kinds of weather. Effective communication has the ability to bring situations to a climax, relieve tension, clarify positions, and encourage meaningful discussions.

When you unleash the power to speak up, you will find the courage to speak out.

If you're not a natural communicator, I suggest you undertake a course and learn the art of conversation because it is an art form, and therefore you should understand the rudiments to ensure your engagements are more compelling and forthright. Once you can freely and confidently speak with others irrespective of their place in your life, you will learn to overcome many barriers, build meaningful relationships, and relay your intentions and feelings in a clear and unambiguous manner.

To make a living from communication and ensure your longevity in a very competitive industry, it's imperative you support the desire with professional instruction. If you decide against this investment, your public speaking career could prove to be the shortest and least impressive in history.

Once you understand the science of communication, you should be unafraid to engage others equally, irrespective of their perceived social standing. Have confidence in yourself, your company, or your product, and establish a competent connection with others on an equal footing.

There is a distinct difference between a good and a great speaker. It lies squarely between an acceptable presentation and one which is impactful and empowering—a memorable and moving delivery given by one who fully understands the importance of effective communication.

A powerful speaker is driven and inspired, exuding a powerful presence—confidence, authority, and personality. This individual is a persuasive communicator—an inspiring leader.

If you are seeking to become a public speaker with the fundamental skills required to support your longevity, the following are a few tips to assist in making even stronger and more impacting presentations:

- *Know your material* inside out and display the supreme confidence of someone who is empowered.

- *Do vocal exercises* before each presentation. Exercise the vocal chords and breathe deeply and evenly to give your voice depth, resonance, and power. Seek the assistance of a vocal coach if necessary.

- *Practice speaking out loud* to become acquainted with the sound of your own voice and to give you authority and confidence.

- *Know the venue*—walk through it if necessary. Get a feel for the stage and select the brightest and most prominent place from which to launch your presentation. This will make you stand out and give you a much stronger appearance.

- *Check out the sound system* to ensure it's working as it should.

- *Walk with confidence when you're introduced.* Enter the stage and approach the audience with open palms and a warm smile which will set the mood. Don't be in too much of a hurry.

- *Keep movements to a minimum* and ensure they have a purpose. Take each step with confidence. Shuffling or unnecessary walking can be distracting. Your movements should be designed to take the audience on a journey.

- *Dress appropriately for the particular engagement* so as not to distract from or demean the quality of your presentation.

- *Try to wear something with pockets.* It provides somewhere to put your hands and will give you a more relaxed persona. Avoid putting both hands in the pockets at any one time or for extended periods as it can make you appear arrogant and detached.

- *Avoid standing* by an open door or window. Outside distractions can take the focus away from your presentation.

- *If using a lectern*, move from behind it as often as possible to prevent it becoming a barrier between you and the audience. Don't use it as a crutch.

- *Use your hands to make points* but avoid over-use through expansive gestures. Don't wave your arms around unless for a specific purpose. Too much movement is a distraction.

- *Keep the presentation simple and impacting* unless you're making a specific presentation where more in-depth information is required.

- *Handouts, visual aids, and overheads* can be very effective in adding depth and quality to a presentation. Make them short, sharp and succinct so as not to bore your audience.
  - Pictures and graphs are acceptable to sustain your material (especially Powerpoint® presentations) and can be supported by written information.
  - No more than four to five short bullet points per page, upon which you can expand vocally.

- *Avoid long pauses between slides in your presentations.* Know your material and move from one topic to the next with a fluid motion to reduce the possibility of audience boredom and disinterest.

- *Fill any voids or blind spots with conversation and questions.* If there are any hiccups with equipment or you go blank for a moment, take a breath, smile at the audience, and perhaps ask a question. Think of an appropriate story to fill the space.

Effective communication crosses all boundaries. When you learn to get your message across to others clearly and concisely, there is no room for doubt or misinterpretation.

Make sure your information is powerful, interesting, and upbeat. Keep it relevant so your audience can concentrate on you rather than spending excessive time reading, writing notes, or daydreaming. It will detract from the power of the message you're delivering. If they become disinterested, you run the risk of disconnecting and losing them. You might not be offered another occasion to present.

In the art of communication, it's imperative you listen with your heart and your head. You will begin to hear the clear, crisp messages being imparted and respond accordingly. It enables you to continue your forward journey with clarity, vision, and purpose.

Blocks are removed and confidences confirmed as you gain a greater understanding of what's occurring and build bridges between yourself and others in your personal and professional lives.

When you learn to communicate effectively with others,
your life will begin to evolve into a very productive and
meaningful existence as you remove the barriers and build
trust with family, friends, and business associates.

LESSONS LEARNED

1. Communication is paramount in all aspects of our lives.

2. Effective communication involves three fundamental components.
   - What you say (7 percent)
   - The way you say it (38 percent)
   - The overall package (55 percent)

3. An effective communicator is also a good listener.

4. Always engage an audience and make yourself and your subject interesting.

5. Ask open-ended questions to receive effective responses.

6. Understand the nature of and reason for communication.

7. Recommendations follow great presentations.

8. Effective communication is fundamental to growth and development.

9. Good written communication is as important as the spoken word.

10. Effective communication breaks down barriers.

11. The workplace requires open channels of communication.

12. A business is like a clock—all parts must work in harmony.

13. Effective communication relieves tension and encourages structured interaction.

14. There is a number of things you can do to empower yourself and ensure your presentation is successful, enlightening, and powerful.

15. Effective communication breaks down barriers and builds meaningful relationships.

16. Listen with your heart to truly hear the message being communicated.

Chapter 12

THE GENTLE ART OF PERSUASION

For the art of persuasion to be truly effective, you must convince others that what they have seen, heard, and felt is absolutely true. While you simply say it's so, there is room for doubt. When others see it, say it, and believe it, suddenly it becomes reality.

The most powerful, influential, and persuasive word in communication is *yes*. It opens doors, maintains friendships, starts businesses, erects buildings, and creates infrastructure. It sells products, empowers dialogue, brings down barriers, and permits successful negotiations to commence and conclude.

To begin and continue a successful business, understand how to persuade others to respond *yes* to you and your products. This means having confidence in who you are and the business you control. That's the first step.

Persuasion and influence are true art forms and can be easily learned, especially when the success of your business depends upon your ability to convince others to see value in you as an entrepreneur, know the worth of your products, and respect and support your point of view.

The time is right to master the empowering world of effective communication and grasp the intrinsic importance of negotiation. This knowledge will add real value to you as an individual and an entrepreneur and empower your overall business as an ongoing successful enterprise.

> The word yes is fundamental to any successful outcome. Learn to communicate it effectively and doors will begin to open.

There's no doubt that learning to influence others is an art form. Some individuals are born sales people; others struggle to push their own barrow and talk up their business, no matter how good it might be. It has to be done, no matter who you are or what your business might be. It's a much easier alternative, in the early stages of your business, than paying someone to do your talking for you. That can come later when the business flourishes.

There are several steps to assist in influencing others in regard to your point of view and stimulate the growth of your client/customer base. They have stood the test of time and are used by many business leaders to increase their bottom line:

First and foremost, lead by example. Be a light for others to follow. Develop a high level of integrity in every contact you have with the world and the way you carry on your business. This also includes obvious brand credibility.

In today's market, there's enormous competition, and with it comes the very real possibility that you won't succeed if you don't give yourself the edge as part of your plan of action.

Gain a very sound understanding of your business. Always remember the reasons why you started and just how/why others will want to be a part of your venture. It's not imperative to have an intimate knowledge of human behavior, but instill in your business/product those special elements which will attract others to it.

Learn to get into the heads of your customers/clients; know why they behave as they do and what attracts them to you and your brand. Capitalize on that vital information.

Give credit and praise. Acknowledge when others mirror your positive behavior. It will reveal you as a warm, courageous, and approachable entrepreneur/manager and serve to attract others to your brand. This will inevitably increase the bottom line.

Allow your business to exhibit a positive, fresh, effervescent air. People will automatically be attracted to a person, business, product, and/or idea which is fresh, innovative, and welcoming. It presents an image with which they feel comfortable.

Always be approachable and remain visible. When people can see you and have access to your warmth, wisdom, creativity, ideas, and knowledge, they will feel a part of the enterprise and be more likely to support you as you grow and develop.

Stay calm and professional at all times. Even in stressful times, stand your ground, though don't be afraid to concede points. When you exude a calm, professional, and approachable manner, you will appear conciliatory and accessible. This can only serve to increase your professional standing and credibility.

If you run blogs or encourage feedback, never take negative comments personally. Customers often use this medium as a means of anonymous derision. These comments are frequently unfounded and a simple knee-jerk reaction to an isolated incident often unrelated to you or your business.

Remain calm and objective and accept any reasonable feedback as a gift from the universe and respond accordingly.

Screen responses where possible to ensure they are not inappropriate.

Realize errors are a part of growth. This will humanize you when you acknowledge your gaffe. Make the appropriate amendments and/or concessions and continue on the new path.

Be understanding when others make errors. Give some leniency.

Give credit where due and encourage others to stand in the spotlight. You will appear fair-minded, respectful, and considerate if you permit others to take the credit for tasks, words, and thoughts which can reasonably be attributed to them.

Maintain your sense of humor no matter what life throws at you. It's claimed by many that when you laugh, you significantly increase your ability to absorb information because it relaxes you and opens pathways in the brain. Have you ever heard the saying, "Laughter is the best medicine"? It also drastically decreases your stress levels.

There will doubtless be times when you want to scream and pull your hair out: However, when you learn to laugh (or even smile) when adversity comes knocking, the impact will be nowhere near as severe.

It acts as a magnet for customers and clients alike. Remember that there is always sunshine after the storm. Start to chill a little and enjoy your life.

Learn patience and understanding. There will be instances when others will certainly annoy you, but it's important you adopt a non-confrontational approach, especially when opinions differ on a common theme. Others will learn to trust you, from which will grow respect and commitment.

You achieve far more when you work as a cohesive and organized team. You will never please everybody or be friends with everyone—it's human nature.

Your power to influence others lies in your innate honesty and integrity and the credibility you build in the eyes of those with whom you interact.

The quality and power of your persuasion lies in the depth and clarity of your argument. If you are initially convincing and prevailing, you have a strong foundation upon which to build your business. It must also be supported by the superiority and reliability of the products and/or services.

People will be persuaded by the authority and personal touch of a presentation, in contrast to the weight of the facts—though the validity in this aspect should never be overlooked. The manner in which you present yourself in any formal presentation, with particular regard to the integrity you demonstrate in relation to your business/product, will ultimately determine the level of support you can garner and continue to receive.

> The capacity to live a truly inspired life is within each and every one of us. We need only believe.

If someone wants to believe in you/your product and become a customer/client, you must be persuasive in a number of areas:

- You can professionally and confidently deliver what they want with no question or hesitation.

- They need what you have because you have absolute faith in your product.

- A professional association with you will be a positive step for them to take.

- They will receive enormous benefit from an association with you and your organization/product/services.

You'll never successfully persuade someone of the integrity of your product/service or the value of yourself as a speaker (or confident and capable business of any type) if you don't believe in yourself and the power of your own argument and/or presentation.

It's imperative that you be confident of who you are and what you stand for. Let there be no doubt about your positive and proactive business and yourself as a professional. Exhibit an unerring faith in your principles. You are the brand and therefore *the* ideal ambassador. Learn to shine and exhibit that "can do" attitude. It marks your organization as truly professional, honest, supportive, and customer-oriented—a perfect business card.

> Never wait for your successful and abundant future to come to you—it will never find its way.

A very positive and logical viewpoint offered to clients, customers, and prospects will open minds, hearts, and doors to the future. Learn to cautiously exhibit a *yes* attitude in all dealings with others. Don't allow negativity to overshadow your push forward. You're building a business (brand) and your hard work and sensible approach should reflect this notion.

Be positive, upbeat, honest, and forthright in every aspect of your personal and professional life. You'll have a far greater chance of bringing others around to your point of view and obtaining their full support for your idea/product/business.

Credibility is difficult to build but so easily destroyed through inappropriate, thoughtless, and deceitful words and actions. In all you do and say, you are representing the brand you seek to build. Your everyday approach to others will be an indication of your overall quality as a business associate, supplier, speaker, coach, manager, partner or employee.

On your journey to your final destination, never
allow the negative energy of others to impact upon
or adversely influence the path you take.

LESSONS LEARNED:

1. The most powerful word in communication is yes.

2. There are specific steps to influencing others:
    - First and foremost, lead by example.
    - Gain a sound understanding of your business enterprise.
    - Give credit and praise, acknowledging when others mirror your positive behavior.
    - Allow your business to exhibit a fresh and positive air.
    - Always be approachable and remain visible.
    - Stay calm and professional at all times.
    - Don't take blog or feedback comments personally.
    - Realize errors are a part of growth.
    - Give credit where due; invite others to stand in the spotlight.
    - Maintain a sense of humor no matter what you encounter.
    - Learn patience and understanding.

3. Learn to carry a smile as often as possible; it acts like a magnet for business associates/clients.

4. A credible presentation is a powerful and persuasive tool.

5. Learn to smile to reduce stress, increase your information absorption levels, and assist you to recognize opportunity.

6. The depth of your influence lies in the power of your logic.

7. To persuade others, you must believe in the value of your own argument.

8. Exhibit a 'yes' attitude in all your dealings with others.

9. Don't allow a bad attitude to overshadow your forward motion.

10. Be positive, honest, and forthright in your endeavors to influence others.

11. Credibility is difficult to build but so easy to destroy.

Chapter 13

ADDITIONAL STREAMS OF INCOME

Once you commit to personal success, you close the
door on mediocrity and move your life to a completely
new plane of existence. This is a wonderful place where
your senses are heightened and your focus is on a
higher and more personal level of greatness.

When you develop your plan and start to become aware of opportunities as they arise, never simply dismiss additional ideas and information as irrelevant. They very often form the basis of those very lucrative *additional streams of income* (ASI) and become ideal means to capitalize on associated opportunities with the ability to build ongoing wealth.

Consider every idea you get because, should they prove fruitful, you will continue to advance your financial success. They will only be of benefit if they are kept and considered. All ideas, notions, proposals, and schemes can have enormous possibilities.

Never dismiss an idea. It could be the one which opens the door to incredible success and prosperity.

Many people refer to this aspect of accumulating wealth as *passive income* because it works quietly (passively) behind the scenes, increasing your wealth.

This is a major contributing factor to the continued wealth creation of many entrepreneurs. They use various web-related tools such as additional websites, *joint venture partnerships* (JVPs), and affiliate programs to increase their income twenty-four hours a day, seven days a week.

The Internet is constantly changing, and with it the many systems for improving your website and updating your marketing tools. In addition to the occasional revision and tweak to keep your website fresh and relevant, you should also pay attention to any new Internet trends so you can keep abreast of the changes and operate your website as a powerful and innovative tool.

Passive income streams are in fact aggressive forms of accumulation because they constantly work for you—building your image, establishing your strong credibility, and increasing your bank balance even while you sleep. They are outstanding ways to continue on the road to financial freedom.

> When you release the inner fear and open the window of opportunity in your life, you allow the winds of change to bring success and empowerment into your psyche.

Additional streams of income technology is a brilliant concept because when you master it and have quality products to release into the marketplace, almost immediately your ideas, projects, and creativity are working for you.

It gives you the ability to build additional financial wealth from a variety of areas. At any time of the day or the night across every corner of the world, others have access to you and your market, thanks to the power of the Internet. There is certainly nothing passive in this action, especially when it is supported by a sound marketing strategy.

When you decide to adopt an ASI program, examine the many business opportunities available that require little work apart from setup, yet with rewards which can be outstanding for business growth and financial return. It might involve obtaining products and services from another part of the world where they can be produced cheaply (while maintaining the product/service integrity) and resold in your country and elsewhere at a profit.

Whatever enterprise you undertake, you must add value across all areas of the business and understand the necessity to make your products work for you.

Depending upon your enterprise and if you are truly serious about making money and expanding your wealth, I again stress the importance of a website. It's now a critical international tool of choice. It provides the ability to market and sell yourself and your various businesses/products to an ever-growing global customer base with a voracious appetite for value.

> When you're true to yourself and your dreams, the impact you have on others and the world will be in line with what you desire to manifest in your own life.

Every competent marketing tool you use adds depth and value to your products/services. The more channels you develop, the greater your ability to create wealth and enhance your financial freedom. It all adds momentum to your forward motion.

For instance, as a coach or speaker you advertise your skills and experience through your own website (and various industry related blogs and social media sites, with links back to your site). You have an information page which explains your products and services. You have a "shopping cart" where people download their chosen products—information, books, manuals, and e-books. They all support and enhance your credibility and expertise.

With experience, you'll progress to blogs, webinars, seminars, CDs, DVDs, MP3s and merchandise. With your extended profile and newfound "expert status" will also come public speaking, training, and seminar opportunities on a global scale. Suddenly, the prospects are virtually endless. You now find yourself with these extraordinary new avenues for additional income closely associated with your original idea and others you've developed to increase your wealth.

As you grow, you can invite other complimenting businesses to place advertising banners on your site to attract more traffic. In turn, you can advertise on those sites which will assist your business to grow. You might also introduce *affiliate programs* where other like-minded entrepreneurs can sell your material through their sites on a reciprocal basis. You can also add value by "free bonuses" (cost-effective product), and suddenly your material is found in an increasing number of hands across the globe, thereby elevating your status as an expert in your field and further expanding your ability to increase your wealth.

You also assist this growth process (see Chapter 10: "Sales and Marketing Knowledge") through the many networking sites and blogs. They, too, help to develop your authoritative presence. Offer regular information, tips, strategies, and programs for others to follow. Your mailing list will grow.

With time and assistance, you'll find potentially endless ways to increase your business through the power of the Internet. If you have little or no experience, these aspects of potential additional income should be discussed with a website/Internet marketing specialist. Be careful in your choices.

These ideas can accompany almost any proposal you can possibly imagine. If you are a handyman, small/medium/large business owner, or entrepreneur and want to substantially grow your business, you can use the Internet to build on your momentum by branching into related and relevant topics/products to assist what you do. When the ASI system is developed and used effectively, it can greatly improve your finances and help extend your client base. It has the propensity to deliver you and your business/product to an entirely new, more diverse, and suddenly stronger and much wider customer base.

There really is no limit to the possibilities of additional income when you apply your mind and skill and think laterally. You have endless ways to make money and increase your customer base with products/services which are relevant to your sphere of expertise, professionally produced, informative, and fully supported. How cool is that!

As new days bring new challenges, so too new thoughts bring fresh, new, and incredible ideas and opportunities.

If you are a speaker you will have engagements, seminars, and personal appearances where you should use the add-on products as "back of room" (BOR) sales. Hype is created by your presence and powerful delivery. At the end of the presentation, attendees purchase the material to further assist their development. The opportunities are endless and the additional income can be quite extraordinary. It's also an ideal way to build your client list.

Business owners, entrepreneurs, speakers, and personal/business coaches—in fact, anyone with a commercial spirit and passion for what they do—can begin to develop and revolutionize products when they understand the limitless power of the Internet. While there will be an initial outlay, it will pale into insignificance as you begin to see the fruits of your labor.

With some tweaking and occasional updates as you gather momentum, your products will continue to keep you in the mind of the public, at the same time providing a steady income stream into the future. This is truly a win/win situation.

> Your life is like a book and you the author. In order to have an ending where you embrace success and happiness, you must create it.

An *ASI focus* means you don't need nerves of steel to venture into unknown places, cautiously trying your hand at something vastly different from what you're presently doing, which could stifle passion. Simply build on and expand your current skills and experience. As your confidence grows, so too will your ability to build more wealth.

Take advantage of all aspects of advertising, sales, and marketing regarding those products and services you currently know but perhaps at the present time are unable to capitalize on.

In simple terms, you remain focused on what you're doing and, through drive and commitment, allow the products to sell themselves. Keep a constant eye on your market and apply some affirmative action from time to time to ensure the sales and marketing programs you've employed are doing the right job and giving you a better than reasonable return on your investment.

New products and innovations should be swiftly brought to the notice of your existing and prospective clients through the various communication channels you've created. Your regular blogs and Internet mailing list are very good ways to remain fresh in the minds of your clients and inform them of changes and additions within your business.

> Keep your focus on where you're going. Stop worrying about where you've been.

Update, improve, and expand your products at those times when you believe they need a makeover. Always stay on top of any changes within your sphere of expertise and make modifications when appropriate, so you too remain relevant and professional.

As you gain confidence and your experience grows, so too will your line of additional products. You begin to see your business in a whole new light and better understand your market.

Now you can more easily gauge the ever-increasing possibilities for growth. Suddenly the future looks so much brighter.

There is only one person in this world who truly matters—you!
Until you can maintain a real love and respect for all you are
and everything you do, your life will never be in vivid color.

LESSONS LEARNED

1. Always be on the lookout for opportunities that will arise around you.

2. Opportunities can increase your success and prosperity as you become more successful.

3. The Internet presents some great prospects for growth and innovation.

4. Products which enhance your business are great sources of supplementary revenue.

5. Additional streams of income (ASI) allow you to make money while you sleep.

6. Affiliate programs also offer tremendous opportunities for increased income.

7. Motivational speakers, coaches, and leaders are very adept at using ASI.

8. ASI allow you to capitalize on your skills and experience to create extra earnings.

9. Ensure your products are always relevant to capitalize on financial opportunities.

10. Commit to social networking and blog sites to grow your presence as an expert.

11. Continue to be on the lookout for progressive ways to grow your income.

12. Be aware of your products and keep them updated to remain innovative and relevant.

Chapter 14

THE VALUE OF EFFECTIVE TIME MANAGEMENT

You can never buy, sell, or trade your time. It remains
an elusive yet priceless commodity with the capacity
to add value, depth, and meaning to your life.

Success depends largely upon your ability to manage your time effectively. It's a true consumable that you cannot save. It's not a commodity that can be put on the back burner until tomorrow. This means allocating time wisely and prioritizing your tasks according to your plan of action. Give sufficient time to the most critical tasks—those which are of the highest value to you (and which are time sensitive).

No matter what you do in life, it all takes time—whether that's sleeping, working, or pursuing leisure activities—and therefore, prioritizing is a must if you are to achieve significant milestones.

Time should never be wasted but rather treasured and, like water, used wisely. Once you master this ability and understand the significance, you'll know what it means to embrace a much higher level of success as you begin to complete specific tasks within a reasonable time frame. This frees you up to become more efficient and effective in completing further jobs.

Family members and friends should always be high on your list of priorities in regard to the allocation of time. Ensure sufficient time is given over to building and nurturing relationships so they don't become fragile and subsequently disintegrate. It can and will also add stability, clarity, and purpose to your life.

Connections with children, spouses, parents, relatives, neighbors, social contacts, and business relationships (and even strangers) are all fundamental components of your personal and professional growth and development.

Effective time management is a tremendously powerful and necessary tool for eliminating procrastination from your life and expediting success.

You should never forsake those who form a crucial aspect of your world nor underestimate their value and importance in your life. It's central to balance and harmony across all aspects of your existence. Take the time to connect and, where necessary, reconnect.

To build your plan for a successful life and remain focused on your goals, the first and most fundamental requirement is to decide on a time frame and ask yourself, "On what do I need to focus and what positive action is required over the next week, month, year (and even five years) to complete this task and get me from where I am to where I want to be?"

It stands to reason, therefore, that when you give sufficient time over to thinking the plan through, it will save you an enormous amount of future effort (and invariably time) when you are working through your plan.

From this process you will begin to set priorities. This means constant evaluation of your plans and associated actions, ensuring you make the best possible allocation of time to the most important tasks. Put in the required effort according to the projections you've set.

The first essential tool in setting priorities is the ability and willingness to do so. This means being prepared to constantly evaluate your plans and instigating any necessary changes.

> Life's path is rarely paved with gold, though the opportunities to find treasure are endless.

In spite of your enormous talent and creativity, your efforts will amount to very little if you don't learn to prioritize. If you fail to complete tasks, it will impact your drive and motivation. It will also greatly affect your bottom line. There is, of course, a way to begin the process which will assist you to remain on top of your tasks and continue to move systematically from one to the other. It's a matter of adopting a disciplined strategy for improvement.

In addition to my journal, I use what I term my effective "1-2-3" method of prioritizing my schedule to make it easier to manage. It allows me to more efficiently apportion my time. Besides my empowering diary/journal entries, I also include daily, weekly, and monthly tasks divided into specific folders according to their weight and importance.

This is how it works: The first are the "1" or mandatory tasks, critical to ongoing business matters. The financial and commercial ramifications are genuine and time sensitive. Given their high priority, wherever possible allow extra time for their completion according to urgency. These should be completed before you move on to the less important jobs.

When you have more than one (associated) task, they can be numbered 1-i, 1-ii, 1-iii, etc.

> Time is never-ending. It lives and breathes in every one of us. Use it wisely and it will be your best friend.

The second are the "2" tasks. Some weight and significance is attached, but they are clearly not as time sensitive as the preceding "1" group. There are some minor consequences associated with failure to meet them, though not as impacting as the "1" category.

The third group is the "3" tasks—generally socially oriented, completed when/if time permits. These are more fun/leisure pursuits with no real consequences or ramifications for failure to complete.

If you use a computer-based diary or reminder system, you can still quite easily use the same labeling process. This also applies to your electronic diary/organizer.

Make prioritization a habit so you establish and maintain some semblance of order in your daily life. It will save time, help your business run much smoother, and streamline daily activities.

When you become more organized and learn to effectively prioritize, it will significantly reduce your stress levels.

A clear time line helps to more effectively set specific goals and tasks and assist you to keep on top of your to-do list. It can also act as a structured record of your tasks/jobs/achievements. You can look back each day, week, month, and year to see just how far you've come.

Organization across a reasonably strict timeline enables you to gauge your success in capitalizing on opportunities as they arise. I never encourage anyone to be focused 100 percent of the time because it takes away much of life's spontaneity.

> Your future is like an immense ocean—vast and unexplored—yet it holds immense possibilities if you only take the time to believe in your own ability and push out optimistically from the shore on a charted course.

I use the following seven points to assist in compiling my to-do list:

1. **Adopt the KISS (Keep it Simple Sunshine) Principle** to reduce the possibility of discouragement with minor setbacks. Make your lists simple, whether you hand write them in your journal or record them in one of a variety of computer based programs.

2. **Apply sub-headings where appropriate** such as Introduction, Tips and Guidelines, Immediate Action Required, Ongoing Action, More Attention Necessary, Incidentals, etc.

3. **Use an "Additional Items Component"** on your list. This allows you to include last-minute things which arise during the day, and it assists you to keep up with your tasks.

4. **Limit the number of tasks** so the list doesn't become overwhelming. I generally include up to twelve, spread across the folders and time lines. This is manageable and doesn't deter me. If you're diligent, there are fewer tasks left over for the following day.

5. **Use due dates/times** against each item, which will assist with accomplishments and make sure every entry is completed by the specified time allocated.

There's no time like the present to give life and meaning to the future.

---

6. **Highlight your accomplishments** by capitalizing, bolding, or with a marker. This enables you to keep abreast of your achievements. It serves to heighten your confidence and keep you on track.

7. **Use time effectively.** Make the best use of your available hours and prioritize according to urgency (refer to the "1-2-3" method on preceding pages). This doesn't mean major tasks require more work, time, or effort. Learn to be a smarter and more efficient operator.

How you choose to respond (or not) could have consequences. Therefore, it makes perfect sense to expend the greatest effort on the more functional (and pressing) tasks and those which will give you the most abundant return.

This assists you to identify the critical tasks and provide the best results from your efforts.

Never underestimate the value of good time management. It has the ability and capacity to put value into your every day, which can accelerate your success.

The more important the task, the greater will be the consequences of your success or failure. The undertaking should therefore embody more effort and focus. This is making the best use of your time and assisting in managing the tasks professionally.

Be determined to complete tasks. This goes hand in hand with prioritizing because they're linked. You must decide the best use of your time and then organize and plan your day/week/month accordingly. If you have this in the forefront of your mind, it will serve to keep you on track and continue to fire your enthusiasm.

Learn to tackle jobs as they arise and don't be distracted from the final objective. This is called "single handling," where you begin and complete tasks expeditiously to significantly cut down on the time you waste going back and forth.

With this system you need not re-familiarize yourself with any aspects of the matter, but can apply your total focus for those moments you give to the completion of the things which are important.

Every moment in time is a fabulous place to be, even though it is over in a breath. It leaves a lasting impression on us and our lives, and as a collective, moments have the capacity to lay the platform for an incredible future.

There is no need to recover momentum or pick up where you left off when you approach your work with this in mind. Instead, you apply your total dedication to particular tasks until completed. This is how awesome achievements are accomplished and successes realized.

To become an effective time manager, you can take a course or check on the boundless information available. You then have to practice; this could mean being a little ruthless (yet practical) with your time. Remain determined to finish specific tasks within the time allocated. It takes a great deal of practice to become an accomplished time manager, but when you have the skills they serve you exceptionally well in all aspects of your daily life.

> You must not allow the sands of time to blow aimlessly about your door. Gather them up and use them in your hour glass as you forge new horizons. Time waits for no one.

As you learn to master time, you take control of your life and put meaning and direction into tasks. Time management becomes indispensable and a critical exercise in general life building and creating stability in your business. You gain a more sound understanding of the enormous value it has in every aspect of your daily existence.

Since time immemorial nothing has ever been achieved through hesitation. Whether working, studying, or undertaking some leisure pursuit, when you understand the value of time and the impact it has on your life you will begin to cherish it. You'll closely follow your accomplishments according to the amount of time you spend supporting, accelerating, and nurturing all your positive actions, thoughts, words, and emotions.

> An effective time manager has a clear and unimpeded vision of the future, with the drive and determination to make the most of every moment.

Time management, like any other success tool, is a learned process. It takes effort to become a master. You cannot afford to become a slave to time. It should instead be at your beck and call. It's a critical implement which you learn to utilize competently to get you from where you are to where you want to be in the most efficient manner.

If you look at the lives of some of the world's most successful people, past and present, you'll see just how they utilized their time effectively to successfully accomplish tasks and, ultimately, created the ideal existence for themselves and their families. The world's great leaders are masters of time. They have stringent schedules and often are driven by a focused and time-strict team. It is a great tool if you understand it and know the power it has in your life.

> Don't waste time on insignificant pursuits, but put success and abundance firmly in your sights. Whatever you apply your mind to, you can achieve.

Without effective time management, you can never achieve everything you wish to. Procrastination is the enemy of time, because while you are in a period of indecision you will never accomplish everything you have before you. Apply your mind to your future and give purpose and energy to everything you do, without the darkness of hesitancy.

Set your own agenda. Develop plausible time lines within which you work conscientiously. Your plan should enable you to have limit lines for various tasks and use past successes as basic guides to future endeavors. You must always be decisive and driven with focus and determination.

Your desire for success must always be greater than the power of indecision or doubt, which can and will creep into your life and attempt to derail your plans. This can infiltrate your world from inherent beliefs, bad experiences, and/or the negativity and narrow-minded view of others. It can also be a simple response to your own doubts and fears.

> Every hour of the day need not be filled with accomplishments, but every accomplishment will inevitably be filled with your hours. Make them count.

Effective time management will enable you to remain ahead of the game, plan, organize, and set achievable agendas. You can always alter time lines, provided you can see the finishing point or at the very least have a good grasp of where you are at any given time in relation to your goals and the tasks required to achieve them.

With a structured time management plan, you will begin to worry less about specific tasks and your stress levels will be reduced. It won't happen immediately. It takes a great deal of practice but is possible with dedication and application.

Never underestimate the value of time. It can be your best friend or worst enemy. If you utilize it correctly and have respect for its value, time will assist you in everything you do. Manage it effectively and use it in unison with your other fundamental tools for success; you will eliminate much of the doubt and cloud from your life.

Learn to manage time and you learn to prioritize, achieve goals, and set aside moments to enjoy the finer things life offers.

Time management allows you to embrace change and move forward with your plans and dreams for success. It's a tool necessary to comprehend and appreciate the intrinsic value of your effort, graph your journey, and move systematically forward according to your vision.

It adds value and depth to your life because it assists you to become focused, driven, and much more competent and accomplished. You see life in a completely different light and gain a much deeper understanding of yourself, your path, and the horizon which beckons.

Everything will become clearer and much more enticing when you begin to master time. Don't allow it to enslave you.

There is a time and a place for everything positive and empowering in your life. The time is now and the place is wherever you envisage it to be. You need only make up your mind exactly what you wish to fill it with.

Time management is an age old skill, designed for you to get the most and the best out of every day. Use it wisely and confidently.

LESSONS LEARNED

1. Effective time management is fundamental to success.

2. Apportion time according to the critical nature of tasks.

3. There are seven points to assist in implementing a functional to-do list:
   - Adopt the KISS (Keep it Simple Sunshine) principle.
   - Apply sub-headings where appropriate.
   - Use an "Additional Items Component."
   - Limit the number of tasks on your list.
   - Use due dates/times.
   - Highlight your accomplishments.
   - Use time effectively.

4. Every action has consequences; therefore, prioritizing makes professional sense.

5. Nothing is ever achieved through indecision.

6. Learn a "single handling" approach to your tasks to more rapidly accomplish them.

7. Time management is a learned process.

8. Never be a slave to time.

9. Apply energy and focus to everything you undertake.

10. Set time lines and work conscientiously toward your goals.

11. Never underestimate the value of time.

12. Time management allows you to move forward and embrace change.

13. Effective time management adds depth and value to your life.

14. Gain a deeper understanding of yourself, your path, and the horizon.

15. Time assists you to comprehend and appreciate the intrinsic value of your own plan.

16. Effective time management adds value and depth to life.

17. Everything becomes clearer as you begin to master time.

Chapter 15

THE NECESSITY FOR SAVING MONEY

Always seek and maintain the value and integrity in every situation.

No one should ever underestimate the value and importance of saving. So many people are totally focused on making money; they give little or no thought to this crucial aspect of longevity and security. They often find it becomes easier to accrue finances as confidence and self-esteem grow. They can suddenly capitalize on their talents and creativity and the money begins to flow into their lives.

However, when it comes to saving they let themselves down because they don't understand the fundamental necessity for this crucial aspect of accumulation, which is a discipline requiring action and dedication. Once mastered, it will flow into other areas of life.

You need to build a wall between your increased earnings and increasing costs. When more money is coming in, you will invariably begin the process of improving your lifestyle, and the spending can often get out of control.

Treat your life as a business—your own personal economy. Keep costs under control to improve the bottom line. Cast a keen eye over spending, especially non-essential expenses. Curb spiraling costs and institute a sensible budget, because even if you suddenly find you have an abundance of income you can easily become overwhelmed and think it will last forever. It rarely does if you are reckless and irresponsible.

Your budget should include all monthly incomings and outgoings; try to limit your expenditure to that financial plan. Know exactly where your money is going and be responsible. You will begin to see a marked improvement in your savings.

The fact that you have money doesn't mean you have to spend it thoughtlessly. There are some sensible steps you should take to keep that extra money in your life. I advise clients to enlist the assistance of a financial advisor or specific business coach to help with a sensible plan for saving and investment.

To become financially secure, there is a requirement to put a certain amount of money aside (for those "rainy days"). Even if you suddenly find you have an abundance of income, it's too much of a temptation to allow spending to get out of hand. You need to institute a plan for the lean times. They will come.

> When anything you do for others has an expectation attached, everything you receive will have a limitation.

Parents, guardians, mentors, teachers, and others in authority should institute a "savings mentality" in young people so they develop with a responsible attitude to money. As income grows, so too should financial responsibility, and as the young move into adulthood the advice they receive and their foresight to accumulate assists them to develop a sound understanding of saving and investment.

This is made easier when you're adept in your field through gaining knowledge and developing your skills. Once again, look at the budget across all facets of your life. The better you become at what you do, the more money you can see coming into your life. Know your products, understand the tasks in which you are involved, and put total energy and focus on your determination to succeed.

This could involve reading, attending seminars, and taking courses to polish your skills. Once you become competent in your job, your confidence will grow. You will then have more money coming in. The process of accumulation should begin in your early years and continue in earnest as your financial security increases.

> Your capacity to make money is a measure of your ability to competently and confidently manage.

From the outset, I discuss with clients the importance of introducing a savings initiative to their overall plan of action. I encourage them to put aside as much as ten percent of their income as a buffer for the lean times which will (and have) invariably come.

It certainly is not a huge amount but can mean the difference between financial buoyancy and that other less than ideal place. Should your earning capacity be diminished, you become ill or for some reason find yourself unable to work or earn that same substantial income, you could fall into difficulty.

It means taking ten percent of your entire income. If you have additional streams (ASI), take the percentage from all areas. This also includes any inheritance, windfall, or other incidental monies. On face value it might seem excessive, but remember that by the time you are earning a high income, you will be enjoying an enviable lifestyle which you will wish to maintain.

There might be times when you will not be earning the same high and steady income. You'll be glad of the buffer you put aside. Ten percent is not such a huge amount as to impact on your lifestyle. It will soon become a habit when you do it every day.

If you're the main bread winner in your household, bear in mind that any income lost can seriously impact the family. When you think ahead and put the small amount aside, it will become a financial lifeline for any contingency.

> Ensure you never waste tears on what you're unable to change. Instead, smile and have gratitude for those things you can.

I advise clients to break up their income into a variety of components. This is often difficult to do when you begin earning a great deal. You forget the rules of responsible fiscal management and often embark on a reckless spending spree. The short-term ramifications might not be as potentially devastating as those in the long term if you continue on this path without a serious plan to keep track of your finances. You must become fiscally responsible.

Having money is important to your continued existence; that much is obvious. Keeping it, however, is critical to your future. By taking a few sensible steps, you can ensure your future and lifestyle are relatively secure.

As a rule of thumb, I advise clients on the following points to secure and maintain the desired lifestyle:

- Up to 10 percent of income put aside as future savings. This can include additions to superannuation, managed funds, savings accounts, and even property investments.

- Up to 65 percent aside for taxation, payroll, and other pecuniary requirements.

- Up to 15 percent aside for general household maintenance and day-to-day living.

- I also give a percentage to charity (which can vary according to income).

By sticking to this rule and making it a habit, you too will develop the confidence and the ability to take calculated risks, which in turn will have the capacity to expand your income generating opportunities.

It does depend upon your income and personal circumstances, but if you adopt a sensible budget it will help you to save money and still live very well.

Before you do anything, seek sound financial advice from a professional.

> If you stand and wait long enough, life will deliver you something. However, if you have no dream, vision, or plan in place, it will likely be an opportunity you neither recognize nor appreciate.

Knowing you have a strong savings plan in place—and substantial reserves put aside to assist during those periods when the sun may not shine brightly in your life—will give you the determination and drive to move forward with confidence. It could just prevent you from falling into debt and losing that lifestyle you've worked so hard to maintain.

In periods of crisis when many of the factors which impact you are out of your control, it remains imperative you have a sound financial safety net in place to assist in weathering the storms. It could last for some considerable time. If you're prepared, the effects will be far less devastating and you will find it easier to ride out the situation.

I can't stress enough the importance of engaging the services of a qualified financial planner or accountant if you have any doubt whatsoever in relation to your finances or you want to ensure your savings program is sound. The advice will help you to instigate a strategic program to help in achieving a state of financial freedom.

I am a money magnet, and every day huge sums flow
constantly and effortlessly into my life and my bank account.

LESSONS LEARNED

1. Never underestimate the value and importance of saving.

2. Wherever necessary, put a budget in place and stick to it.

3. Treat the whole of your life like a business and manage it wisely.

4. Seek the assistance of a financial advisor or business coach to create a sensible savings plan.

5. Always put a certain amount of money aside for "rainy days."

6. Understand the necessity for accumulating finances.

7. Put energy and determination behind your focus to succeed.

8. Make saving an integral part of your plan of action.

9. Put aside a percentage of your total income as a buffer.

10. Reduced income has the capacity to severely impact your family and lifestyle.

11. Never forget the rules of continued financial freedom:
    - Up to 10 percent of income put aside as future savings.
    - Up to 65 percent for taxation, payroll, and other pecuniary requirements.
    - Up to 15 percent for general household maintenance and day-to-day living.
    - A percentage to charity (which varies according to income).

12. Having money is important to your future. Keeping it is critical.

13. Break your income into several sensible components.

14. Make saving a habit.

15. Ensure you always have a financial safety net in place.

16. Before you take any action, seek assistance from a professionally qualified financial planner.

Chapter 16

EFFECTIVE STEPS TO PROBLEM-SOLVING

While I look forward in my life, I allow my past the freedom to
give me the vision to lay the foundation for a brilliant future.

Responses to problems, whether personal or professional, are not pre-ordained. There is no necessity to react as you believe you should, according to the severity or otherwise of the problem. Very often in our response, we're reacting to the symptoms rather than the cause. This will simply mask the problem for a time as it covers the initial impact of the problem on us, which will inevitably resurface.

It was the great Martin Luther King, Jr. who so famously said, "The ultimate measure of a man is not where he stands in moments of comfort and convenience, but where he stands at times of challenge and controversy."[1]

Any responses you engage will have specific consequences. You can choose from an indeterminable series of reactions, any one of which will impact your psyche. You can be introspective, fascinated, happy, frustrated, surprised, focused, contented, determined, frightened, angered, saddened, or driven—and respond accordingly.

Problems are signposts designed to evoke a response and push us into action, ultimately determining the path we take. Endeavor to keep a clear and rational head when you make those choices. Be passionate and determined about the path you want to follow and life you wish to lead.

> Whatever you do in life, do it first for yourself. Once you've climbed that mountain, you will discover within the courage, drive, passion, and determination to do it for others.

Stop and think carefully about how you respond to any problem. It will impact on the degree to which the dilemma touches you, the force it will have on your life, and the resultant direction you take. It's quite important to see the big picture in any problem-solving exercise. Far too often we make the easier choice to simply address the symptom rather than the root cause of an issue. It will resurface because it has not been eliminated. It will continue to impact your journey.

When the problem comes into your life, try to look at it objectively; take time to identify and isolate the cause and set about addressing it. The symptoms will manifest, and it is those that will take your initial attention. Don't focus too much energy in this direction, but rather get to the cause to begin the process of elimination.

You have to actually embark on a course of action after spending time researching, looking, asking, and investigating. Once the cause is discovered, so too will the symptoms. Ensure the answers you uncover are right for your problem and not simply "band aid" solutions, inappropriate in the circumstances. Search out help and assistance where necessary. There will always be someone with the wisdom, skills, and experience to assist you, and the act of brainstorming will provide an avalanche of possible solutions. You must continue to have faith in all your thoughts, words and actions.

> Once you resolve to make this moment the first in a brilliant future, the sun will begin to shine on your life in all its glory and show you the way forward.

It's important to carefully consider every viewpoint offered and each idea which comes to you. Write them all down, put them into different folders, and refer to them as necessary. There will come a time in your search when you begin to unlock your creative flair, and the solutions you devise will be based on the material/ideas/notions you've gathered and a degree of intuition rather than simply originating in a memory of past events.

Continue to look for the positives in any situation. This will give you a far greater ability to keep a clear head. Stop, take a breath, and examine your situation thoughtfully, then look for plausible alternatives to turn the situation around. This is the time to look at the options you've uncovered in your quest to rectify the situation.

Nothing in life is impossible—*nothing!* Far too often we take the path of least resistance and surrender to the initial impact of the problem. We close our eyes and accept the results as inevitable. Rather than sink to an unfathomable depth of despair, find the courage and determination to swim—even if it's against the rising tide of fear and apprehension. In adopting a mindset of hopelessness and failure, you also open yourself to the ravages of negativity.

A problem will never seem as bad tomorrow as it does today, especially when you set about finding solutions. You've put the wheels of achievement into motion and turned your mindset from one of gloom to one of brightness and optimism.

> The measure of the person you are and the success you'll enjoy lies in the drive, passion, patience, and ingenuity you use throughout your life to solve problems as they occur.

At all points in this quest, believe in your heart (and your head) that your problems are only temporary. They are simply obstacles which stop you in your tracks in those moments, as a deviation from a particular path you're traveling. Throughout our lives we all encounter problems we believe are all-consuming. We can see no way out and the gloom and doom of the moment has the capacity to consume us. We're still here. We have a life and we are moving forward with purpose and passion in spite of those crushing problems which stopped us in our tracks during those harsh moments. It's not luck—it's by design, based on focus and determination. We are creating a more plausible and acceptable future, as opposed to the unpalatable alternative.

This action has the capacity to lessen the adverse effect the problem might otherwise have on your life. Look at it from all aspects and refuse to respond with a knee-jerk reaction. When you can look objectively at the problem and devise plausible solutions, you deny it life and substance and crush it so it doesn't manifest in some other form at some time in the future.

> No matter how much pressure you find in your life, if you dig deep for the courage and vision to persist, you'll one day discover that you've become a true diamond.

It's easy to adopt irrational and short-sighted options when you are subjected to stress and momentary hardship; it's human nature. However, life has taught me many wonderful things, and one of those is fundamental in this exercise. Problems are gifts which provide life lessons. They teach us to find the courage and drive to seek out plausible solutions. Problems provide new perspectives on life and new ways of looking at your world. The solutions build your confidence and passion as you move ever forward and relegate the problems to a state of temporary existence.

The journey toward a resolution to problems is like any other you take. You need to know where you're going before you embark. You require a clear and supported plan. Without direction you will have no power or passion. If you don't know where you want to end up, you won't know how to begin and what tools you require to accomplish the journey. As a consequence, you will continue to wander aimlessly. Problems will persist and keep you sidetracked.

> Even the darkest of tunnels has an eventual light at the end.

With your plan and map in your mind, you have a greater chance of a resolution. Don't be rigid in your approach and be prepared to alter your plan according to the path you follow. It will be necessary to adapt to changing conditions, but remain true to yourself and your journey.

As you develop throughout your life and find the drive and persistence to uncover workable solutions to the problems you face, you will become a more confident person. Your passion and persistence will also grow and success will become a more tangible aspect of your life. Don't be afraid to confront problems, and as long as you understand the need for action and a plausible plan, you will greatly enhance your ability to overcome obstacles and empower your life.

> The view you have and opinion you hold of yourself and your life will ultimately determine the type and degree of success you enjoy.

You must learn to take control of those elements in your environment that can negatively influence you in so many ways. Your plan is not necessarily flawed because you have to tweak it. It indicates your willingness to move forward with confidence and make decisions based upon those elements you encounter and the new solutions you uncover.

Follow the steps you need to take to get your life to a position of prosperity. There's no time like the present to realize your capacity to achieve and believe in the power you have to create and maintain a very full and rich life.

Make up your mind to be a powerhouse. Have the courage and determination to stand by the decision you make and see it through.

The plan is the basic blueprint, and as long as you keep the horizon in view, you will continue moving forward with confidence.

Make the changes as you see fit, according to your direction and what you encounter along the way. There's no time like the present to covet an extraordinary future.

NOTES

1.   Martin Luther King Jr., http://americanprofile.com/articles/martin-luther
     -king-jr-quotes-video/

Never be afraid to ask for help and assistance when your problems seem overwhelming and darkness looms. Assistance from those with the experience, skills, and knowledge to elevate you might make the difference between success and the alternative.

LESSONS LEARNED

1. Identify and isolate the actual problem.

2. Separate the cause from the symptoms.

3. Have the big picture and the end result in your mind.

4. Stop and consider your possible responses.

5. Seek assistance and ask questions.

6. Embark on a considered course of action.

7. Contemplate every possible alternative.

8. Understand that nothing is impossible.

9. Believe that your problems are only temporary.

10. Difficulties are blessings and gifts.

11. Give power and life to your positives.

12. The journey to resolution is like any other.

13. A plan and map will give you a greater chance of resolution.

14. Be adaptable, but remain true to yourself.

15. Always keep the horizon in view.

16. Take control of those things which can impact your environment.

17. Continue forward with confidence.

18. Consider the necessary steps and take them.

19. Your plan is your basic blueprint.

20. Make necessary changes and capitalize on all opportunities.

Chapter 17

THE CHALLENGE OF PROCRASTINATION

If you allow procrastination to fill your days, opportunity will no longer come knocking. True fulfilment and abundance will surely elude you.

Procrastination is not an inherent trait and is often undertaken on a subconscious level. It's a learned process and becomes automatic (almost habitual). It can't simply be labelled as laziness, ineptitude, or disinterest. In fact, there is no simple solution and it goes far beyond self-discipline. It's often (though not always) an indicator of a more pressing and deeper physical or psychological problem.

You can certainly hesitate without procrastinating. One is born of a balanced view of all the issues involved, while the other arises from an inherent fear of *something* and even a sluggishness or indifference. When the issues are visible and ramifications apparent, you are ideally placed to make that fair decision

Procrastination implies hesitancy without foundation. To avoid falling into the habit of procrastination, the hesitation should only be momentary until the verdict is reached and you can move forward with purpose.

Procrastinators generally feel at home in their comfort zones where they find familiarity, convenience, and reassurance. It represents an area where priorities can be readily sacrificed to achieve tasks. Procrastinators are often very intelligent and forthright individuals, but they find a kind of comfort in this area of least resistance.

Somewhere in the vastness of the void, tasks can become mixed up—the urgent and unimportant somehow become jumbled. The less crucial and impacting tasks begin to fill the comfort zone where the procrastinator is unable to prioritize. It's an area filled with fear and uncertainty—often from self-confidence issues.

The procrastinator is easily distracted and finds great difficulty in applying discipline to his/her actions. This can prevent the individual from prioritizing and attending to the more pressing matters. The procrastinator can become forgetful and disorganized where feelings of stress and constriction can overwhelm them. They have notes and slips of paper in all manner of places to remind them of those tasks which should be done.

Success is like surfing—to catch that big wave, you have to get on your board and paddle out from the safety of the shore. Let the wave take you in the direction you want your life to go.

It's in this place that tasks are viewed as a collective rather than various stand-alone pieces of the overall puzzle. This adds further weight to the procrastinator's inability to focus on the specifics. Feelings of inadequacy can become severe and drive the individual further into a state of chaos and indecision.

Chronic procrastinators can require professional intervention to change behavior. This can take time and a great deal of effort as they are required to challenge distorted cognitions and eventually change destructive patterns of behavior.

There is often a fear attached to the completion of tasks. The "but what if" and "what then" questions begin to raise their heads. When all tasks are viewed in totality, the whole process can become overwhelming. It forms blocks which prevent the individual moving forward with purpose.

Before procrastination can be overcome, the individual must confront those aspects which put up the blocks. To do this, the individual needs to understand the nature of and reason for the procrastination and realize that the fear and trepidation are unnecessary and can be reduced or eliminated.

You can delay things without procrastinating. We do it every day as we prioritize the many tasks requiring action in our lives. It makes sense to balance our working life through undertaking the most urgent tasks first and systematically completing them as we conscientiously work through the list. We have a responsibility to do this and not simply close our eyes and hope the task will suddenly become less daunting. It won't.

To take a professional approach and adopt a structured and functional system to deal with everyday tasks makes common sense and is crucial to a successful outcome. That's totally different from procrastination.

When you hesitate for no logical reason, it becomes procrastination. It simply invites setbacks, problems and barriers. There are many who have no desire to bring more challenges into their lives and that's quite understandable. However, if they only realized that to adopt some simple steps—among them, the initiation of a system of prioritization—they have the ability to change their entire world. In turn, this has the very real capacity to bring success and abundance rushing into their arms.

When negativity becomes the norm across all aspects of life, it ultimately overshadows productivity and growth, leading to eventual adversity and possible obscurity.

Those who fear challenge and embrace mediocrity would otherwise be at the front of the line, eagerly grasping opportunities once they understood the futile nature of the road they were traveling compared to what could await them. The doors to so many possibilities would open if they only had the courage to love and respect themselves and their abilities and step out of their comfort zones.

Time potentially lost turns into opportunities gained, and suddenly supposed challenges become real life possibilities.

This faith, together with the power of an open mind and an incredible optimism, will assist any individual to recognize and embrace the opportunities that surround them every day. The wonderful times will far outweigh the challenges, and the warm glow of daylight is much healthier and more encouraging than any clouds or darkness. I ought to know!

A diary, journal, or appointment book is excellent for arresting procrastination as long as you use it consistently. It becomes an ideal storehouse for all information to assist in moving forward. This can be done initially in moderation to prevent tasks becoming overwhelming, which can lead to further feelings of discouragement and disappointment. Once you have your diary, also use it as a prompter to assist when you have memory lapses or multiple tasks to do and things to think of on any given day.

> When doubt becomes a major shareholder in your life, procrastination and resignation become your bedfellows.

Powerful and successful people are achievers. They approach tasks and assess problems from all aspects and seek qualified advice and assistance before proceeding. They have a strong self-belief and a confidence which assists them to make informed and calculated decisions. They evaluate situations and use a common sense and very realistic approach to problem solving. They are certainly not procrastinators.

Planning is a fundamental aspect to eliminating procrastination. Begin to plot and organize a program and start the habit of prioritizing through the information you write in your diary. Use it every day and don't be afraid to take it out and check to see you're on track. Record everything that needs to be done and also those things that you've completed. Break the tasks down into manageable components to avoid feeling overwhelmed. This helps to keep those "but what if" questions at bay. It assists you to remain focused and on track.

Your diary should become a daily ritual where you become accustomed to reading your to-do list and marking off each task as you attend to it.

Eliminate procrastination and self-doubt from your life and you have a perfect opportunity for achievement.

There's no doubt that procrastination can rule your life if you give it power. Taking small but sensible steps will allow you to move into a more secure and confident place. Once you begin to eliminate procrastination, your confidence and self-esteem will grow, and you'll find your days are more productive and focused.

Don't make procrastination a solid component of your life. With practice, planning, and organization you can move beyond this void and begin to establish and sustain a more productive and purposeful life.

When procrastination becomes a very prominent aspect
of your life, you signal to the Universe your unwillingness
to believe in your own ability to succeed. Your future
from that point will be filled with doubt and fear.

LESSONS LEARNED

1. Procrastination is not simply laziness or disinterest.

2. It's often a symptom of other more pressing (underlying) problems.

3. Procrastinators have comfort zones.

4. Procrastinators are often very forthright and intelligent individuals.

5. They mix tasks and are often easily distracted.

6. The procrastinator can be forgetful and disorganized.

7. There is often a fear attached to the completion of tasks.

8. Professional help can reduce or eliminate the trepidation.

9. Planning and organizing can assist in eliminating procrastination.

10. Tasks should be broken down into manageable components.

11. The use of the diary should become a daily ritual.

12. Small and sensible steps assist in building confidence.

13. Practice, planning, and determination establish a more productive life.

Chapter 18

EMPOWERING OUR CHILDREN

Our children are our most precious gifts. Through
unfathomable love, support, and encouragement, it remains
our undeniable duty to help them develop the tools necessary
to uncover and nurture infinite success in their lives.

"Give me the child until he is seven, and I will give you the man."[1] This powerful quotation has been attributed to Francis Xavier, co-founder of the Jesuit religious order. He proposed the notion that a person's core belief system evolves in childhood.

If we are to accept this statement, it makes the task of bringing up a well-adjusted young person critically important to any parent/carer serious about their desire to give a child the best start possible in life.

Children are neither a fringe benefit nor an accessory—they are and have always been blessings. They come into our lives with different characters and personalities and require a variety of stimuli to capture, hold, and expand their attention. It's our duty as parents and carers to support, love, and nurture them for their entire lives—without exception.

A child has the propensity to bring enormous joy to a family (including extended) unit. It remains the duty of every parent (and carer) to develop in all young charges the skills necessary to live the best and most empowering life possible. They are individuals, after all, and should be treated as unique and incredibly special.

> Love and support your children no matter what. They are forever the student and you, the teacher. Support and encourage them every day.

This chapter is not meant as a definitive guide on bringing up children. Rather, it is designed simply as an outline of the support and assistance which can aid in creating and developing balanced lives for the leaders of the future.

When we as adults decide to bring success and prosperity into our lives, we should simultaneously develop that same notion in our young people—as long as we don't lose sight of the fact they are children. Their young lives are presented to us as blank canvases. They are pure and clean. They require our assistance, guidance, love, and support to empower their dreams and goals. They should be given every opportunity to grow and develop their own destinies in their own time.

Children come into our lives as a ray of hope and sunshine. They are put into our care so we might lead them along the often dark and mysterious paths to their futures. It's our task to teach them—empower them to be extraordinary in their lives. They bring us immense joy and also teach us many lessons about life (and ourselves). Though it might not always be an easy road to follow, it is rewarding when our days are overflowing with love, respect, and happiness.

Remember the finger paintings—the priceless works of art they produced for us? The nights spent counting the stars and the endless "but why" questions. The giggles and the bubble blowing; the huge hugs and endless kisses. The birthday surprises and bedtime stories about princesses, kings, and castles. The small hand held in yours as you cross the road or for reassurance on that first day of school.

The love and tenderness our beautiful children bring us is beyond calculation; it's beyond words. The warmth they bring to our hearts is priceless and immeasurable.

> Whenever I leave an impression of appreciation, love, and selflessness on those with whom I come into contact, I have provided them with a lesson in humility and a blueprint for personal success.

It's important to tell your children every day you love them and are immensely proud of the good things they do. If they require support and assistance, ensure you offer it without prejudice. Be open in your approach to them and always congratulate them for good work. Their confidence and self-esteem will begin to evolve.

Health and fitness issues also affect our children. We need to ensure they are eating correctly and getting regular exercise. This is the first step in protecting them from a sedentary lifestyle which can lead to many debilitating illnesses.

It's important to remove children from the influence of the computer terminal as often as possible to ensure they get fresh air and exercise. It also breaks the link they have with the machine and gives you time to connect and communicate in a meaningful way. Limit their time on the computer so there is more balance and meaning in their lives.

Take them for a bike ride or a run. Kick a football or swing a bat. Jump on the swings or just sit in the park and talk about their lives and what's impacting them.

There could be times during your child's life when you have to deal with issues of body image—often brought on by media reporting—magazine pictures, peer pressure, and even sibling rivalry. Their lives are bombarded every day of their formative years, and it's important they understand balance.

Deal with it respectfully and patiently, and if necessary seek advice and assistance from professionals. It's paramount you don't respond negatively, which has the capacity to affect your child's self-confidence and feelings of self-worth. They can carry this negativity right through their adult years with some very adverse results.

Children should have boundaries in their everyday lives. When they cross them and their behavior becomes inappropriate or impacts harmfully on others, as a parent/carer it's our responsibility to discuss their behavior rationally and calmly with them.

Parents and carers should refrain from openly criticizing children because there's no such thing as "constructive criticism." It's all destructive and disempowering. We should simply offer advice and in such a way as children are not threatened or feel disconnected. If it's necessary to reprimand a child for certain aspects of behavior, it should never be done in public. It is something which should be handled with tact and diplomacy in a private and non-threatening environment.

> We enrich the lives of our children and positively alter their behavior by treating them with respect and dignity at all times.

Criticizing and chastising children are different things. When behavior is errant and antisocial, young people need to be made aware of the impact of their actions on others and supported and encouraged through the processes of change. It should always be positive and respectful.

Likewise, when we want to praise children for good deeds, it can be done in public. For instance, if a child performs well in a football game or examination situation, is respectful of others, and behaves in a very supportive and positive manner, he/she can be warmly congratulated. The support and encouragement helps build character and confidence and when sustained, coupled with any constructive advice required (as opposed to criticism), the child learns to develop with harmony and respect.

Find balance in your approach to your children so they too can find balance in their lives.

When we watch our children grow, we are generally filled with awe—at their life, passion, determination, purity, and innocence. It brings a sense of achievement when we see them developing into well-adjusted and determined teenagers and on into their young adult years, generally through our loving and caring words and actions.

Our children are a blank canvas and as they become enriched with color, clarity, creativity, and purpose, we have the right to feel proud of our actions when they fully support, encourage, and nurture.

> When your children ask inquiring questions, make sure you give time to answer them with inspiring answers.

Parents are leaders and mentors and should learn the gentle art of persuasion through positive conversation (see Chapter 12). Fairness and a firm yet encouraging approach by parents (teachers, carers and coaches) will assist them to understand the need for tact, respect, and flexibility when dealing with young people so as not to alienate them or adversely impact their self-esteem or confidence.

It's imperative for children to understand the reasons why some decisions are made so they might realize how their actions impact on their own wellbeing and that of others.

Information appropriate to their age and maturity will assist children as they rationalize situations and instigate appropriate behavioral modification in their daily dealings with others. This is where you help with careful and considered responses to their questions and actions. Open and frank discussions are critical to this aspect of their lives; when they know what is expected of them, they can better understand the consequences of their behavior.

> Parents are mentors and therefore lead by example. Without prejudice or selfishness in their thoughts, words, and actions they lay a strong, safe, and substantial path for children to follow.

Children fill our lives with endless promise. How we respond to the challenge of teaching them the qualities of life, will ultimately determine the kind of teenager and eventually adult they evolve into and consequently, the success or otherwise to be found along the path they travel.

As parents, we have the immense responsibility to guide, assist, and support our children so the notion of success and prosperity in their lives becomes a constant and nourishing force for good. From their earliest days, we teach them to communicate effectively. We feed, nurture, and protect them. It's also our duty to show them endless love and affection and teach them right from wrong (in the ideal world anyway). We must also show them how to be successful.

We're compassionate and patient mentors, coaches, and leaders. We nurture and guide our young charges through every aspect of development. Our examples of respect and goodness automatically show them the power of belief, where great things can and do result from dreams, vision, dedication, and application in spite of challenges faced.

When you have children in your life and under your care, it remains your duty to teach our future leaders the skills necessary to make informed decisions and react with compassion, tolerance, and respect. Don't allow prejudice, fear, or narrow-mindedness to destroy their futures.

Don't permit innate fears and biases to overshadow and impact negatively on responsibilities to your children. Your optimistic outlook should assist them to find the drive, determination, faith, and confidence to realize all that's possible in life.

This means giving them the freedom to enjoy their childhood, while at the same time aiding and supporting them with our love, patience, determination, and integrity through the many challenges they face, so they might find their way and embrace prosperity as it rises up to meet them.

In systematically building their confidence, we also encourage them to face challenges on their own terms and deal with day-to-day adversity through a thoughtful and systematic approach.

Through showing them how to deal with disappointment, we instill in them the need for a level-headed approach where balance, courage, and consideration become indispensable tools of trade.

> Stability and a level-headed approach to difficult situations will also provide our children with a very powerful and positive guide to dealing with success and prosperity in their lives.

As an intelligent and mature society, we cannot hope to have empowered adults without inspired and compassionate young people. The challenge lies in finding what passions drive our children and then supporting them on their individual and collective journeys, rather than endeavoring to fuel our own single-minded ideas.

If we embark on the destructive path of vicariously living our (often failed) lives through our children, we will impact negatively on their development. They are individuals with their own personal destinies. They should be nurtured and supported through this entire process. Allow them the time and space to reach for their own stars, whatever they are and wherever they are to be found. We're simply in their lives to love, support, guide, encourage, and protect them on their (own) brilliant journeys to ultimate fulfilment.

It remains our responsibility to keep our children safe from harm and assist them to develop into dependable, intelligent, well-mannered, and honest adults.

As parents and carers, we are role models and should always act in the most appropriate manner so as to leave a positive impression on our young charges. If we do not take responsibility for their spiritual and emotional growth and development, who will encourage, protect, and nurture them? What hope will there be for the future?

> When your children ask questions, ensure you don't trivialize the importance of their inquisitive natures. Give them the time, support, and assistance they need to grow into inspired young adults.

Our children will encounter many obstacles in their lives, as we've done in ours. However, when we give them our unequivocal love and guidance through the challenging times, we can diminish the impact of the many negative influences which will touch them. This is responsible parenting and paramount to the balanced growth of our young people.

When you find the courage to step from the shadow of complacency in your own world, you automatically lead by example. Your positive and results-driven words and actions assist in opening the minds, hearts, eyes, and ears of your children to the infinite possibilities which surround them every day.

There are endless opportunities to infuse the lives of your young charges with the passion to embrace all the positive and inspiring aspects which can fill their lives. In those priceless lessons lie the foundations of infinite success and prosperity.

Our children have dreams. Remember all those years ago when we told everyone we wanted to be a doctor or airline pilot when we grew up? Perhaps a nurse, police officer, or wildlife ranger—the imagination was rampant as we visualized our future dressed in the uniform or doing those things which filled our lives with purpose. We spent hours running around the house in our make believe worlds, dressed as our favorite characters.

Children are like sponges—they soak up everything the environment offers. Ensure you fuel their internal flames with only honest and empowered information.

When we show our children the value of building dreams by developing a plan of action and fueling it with determination and passion, we've begun the important task of creating a sustainable future. Rather than ridicule them for their "silly make believe," we should instead support and encourage their visions.

We must build and nurture their inner strength so they have a solid platform on which to develop their empowered futures. When we encourage our children to do their best at everything they undertake, we should also instil in them the necessity for fair play and integrity in their everyday lives.

Children are not trinkets. They are, however, gifts who add color and depth to our lives. Their growth and development is our responsibility, and we must always look to their welfare with every moral fiber we possess.

As our children evolve, they must also believe beyond question they have the absolute support of their parents teachers, guardians and/or carers. They will find the courage to step from the shadows and find their way in life as long as they know they have our love and support to sustain them. They will develop a purpose and stride forward with determination and confidence as they begin building their futures.

As long as parents/carers remain non-judgmental and always support their young charges, the children will grow up with love, balance, respect, and confidence—the building blocks for life.

NOTES

1.   Francis Xavier, http://preview.tinyurl.com/oyolfnu.

To have strong and courageous children who
can make informed decisions, we must begin by
allowing them to have confident opinions.

LESSONS LEARNED

1. "Give me the child until he is seven, and I will give you the man."

2. A child is neither a fringe benefit nor an accessory.

3. Children are a ray of hope and sunshine in our lives.

4. Tell your children each day you love them and are proud of them.

5. Discuss rationally with your children when their behavior negatively impacts others.

6. There is no such thing as constructive criticism.

7. Praise children in public; it can build confidence and respect.

8. Parents/carers should refrain from public criticism of children.

9. Our children are precious.

10. Children should be shown the need for boundaries.

11. Give them the tools to succeed.

12. Parents are teachers and mentors.

13. Never overshadow young people with your prejudices and fears.

14. Don't try and live your life through your children.

15. Step from the shadows and lead by example.

16. Encourage your children to dream.

17. Reinforce your children's inner strength.

18. Remain non-judgmental and always encourage them.

19. Never lose sight of their spiritual and emotional development.

20. Your love, support, and assistance will give your children all the power they require.

CONCLUSION

*We create darkness and uncertainty in our lives when
we choose to close our hearts and minds to opportunity
as it passes by on the opposite side of the street.*

This book, the first in a rich and empowering series by the author, provides a very powerful introduction to success and your capacity to introduce it into your life. Anything is possible if you work hard and want it badly enough. No doubt your parents always told you nothing was easy and you had to work incredibly hard for everything you get in life. That's still true to a degree, though the pathway has been illuminated by many focused and passionate people.

There are so many more powerful tools available to us, such as the technology offered by the Internet, smart phones, tablets and other communication devices. Everything you need to accelerate the success process is now at your fingertips. The secret lies in knowing where to look and what to look for.

If life was a real pushover, everyone would be doing it. It stands to reason that it takes effort and determination to find success in your world. Life isn't a walk in the park, in spite of the fact that you have a notion of a better life and a solid plan of action. It takes time, effort, and energy to realize the dream of a better life. You have to remain determined to succeed.

Anything in life is possible—provided you plan and organize for it. The chapters of this book uncover the steps necessary to realize prosperity in your life. There's no doubt you'll face challenges every day—personal and professional. There will probably be times when you will wish the world would swallow you up and other days when you stand proudly on the pinnacle as you have many triumphs.

> Once you get out of yourself and into your dream, it will suddenly become your mission.

Every journey begins with that dream of a better life. Without this first step, you'll stay exactly where you are. When you can dream of prosperity, you begin to put the pieces of the puzzle together. You're on your way to an extraordinary new life. Don't let go of the reigns and never surrender your view of the horizon. When the going gets a little tough, always remind yourself why you're working so hard. Develop a thick skin and an even temperament. Remain hungry and focused so your future stays in your own hands. Learn to smile just a little more.

Don't just sit pondering your navel. There's a great deal of work to do. Begin to put the principles into action. Your amazing future will start when you make up your mind to build something great—a future which reflects your desires. An extraordinary life only manifests when the right action is taken with focus and passion.

> Always believe in yourself and have trust in that voice inside, because when you need decisive and life-changing action in your life, the only voice which truly matters is your own.

Each day is a separate step on your journey. Whether small or large, when you're moving in the right direction you are doing what's necessary to grasp success. Every day will be filled with small wins which should be celebrated.

Read this book from cover to cover and use it as a referral each time you need some inspiration. There will be times when you fall off the track. Just simply take a breath, recover, and get back to where you're going. Understand that you are the only person who can live your awesome life. You are also the only one who has that unique voice inside telling you that you're a wonderful, happy, healthy, balanced, and courageous individual.

Step out of your comfort zone on occasion and just go for it. Your detractors will always ask you why—you have to say, "Because I can." There are no reasons to accept mediocrity in life; there are no reasons to accept mediocrity.

If you give up and walk away, you will never know what it means to taste success after challenge. The more times you get knocked down and stand right up again, the more reasons you have to continue on that incredible journey.

Imagine the possibilities!

Never allow the clouds of uncertainty over the life of another to inadvertently cast a shadow across your own success.

EPILOGUE

*An occasional bad day in the great and inspired life of
your making is far better than a good day in a life in
which you're otherwise constantly wallowing.*

Life is an incredible process of metamorphosis. It represents a path of transformation from who you are to who you wish to be (and will become). You have to know that with a positive attitude, clear and unimpeded focus, planning, and determination, new skills, new ways, and a brand new life await you.

Once you hold absolute and unswerving belief in yourself and all you do, you'll be well on your way to embracing a wonderful future. In addition, when you like, love, and respect yourself and all you do to bring yourself into harmony with the universe, you have begun to empower your life and make your destiny clear and unambiguous.

To be at peace you must have faith in all you are and a respect for the goodness which your life embodies. Understand and embrace this critical aspect of your development and allow it to infiltrate all aspects of your life, thereby denying others the ability to negatively impact your existence and derail your journey.

Begin today to cherish every aspect of your world and start the wonderful process of creation. It is incredibly fulfilling and lifts the clouds of apathy from the horizon.

> While we succumb to the negative influence of life as it is, we will forever remain blissfully ignorant of what life really has in store for us.

Ensure you make time to stand back and look at your life. Be immensely proud of how far you've come, what you've accomplished, and how incredible you feel about all your wonderful achievements. There can be no reason to be avaricious or closed-minded. There is always more work to do, goals to be achieved, and successes to be accomplished. Continue your wonderful journey of growth and development.

Design the destiny you want. Set the bar higher to challenge yourself daily. If you rest on your laurels, you become complacent and in that altered frame of mind indicate a desire to accept life as it comes, rather than as you wish it to be and thus create it.

Once you understand that the world and the universe are wonderful places offering opportunities to those willing to open their eyes, put in the effort, and exert themselves, you will find the commitment to see your dreams and goals through. Every day will not be a bed of roses, but the endless opportunities to succeed will present themselves when you open your heart and your mind and welcome them.

Achievement is part of the wonder of life, and even small successes are to be celebrated and congratulated. Allow yourself time to feel good about your life and your many wonderful achievements. Never allow them to pass by without recognition.

> A dream will always reside in the realm of fantasy until you believe in it, become inspired by it, and then take the ultimate step and act upon it.

Remove from your existence those almost crushing and demotivating aspects of your life which are holding you back. Disassociate yourself from the negative people who impact adversely on you. They are toxic and will succeed in poisoning your world and bringing you down if you allow them to reside within your space.

Step out of the darkness (with professional assistance wherever necessary); express your willingness to be the best you can and utilize everything you have at your disposal to create an abundant and successful existence from this moment on.

Begin today and use the power of your mind to create the life you want. If you can dream of incredible success, abundance, happiness, love, wealth, and power—you can achieve it.

When you waste precious time worrying about who you're not and how stagnant your life might be, you'll never have the time, space, or vision to focus on becoming the person you know you can be and set about creating an incredible life.

You have everything you need to live the life of your dreams, so what's holding you back? Open your eyes, then listen with your heart to the voice of encouragement and reason inside. It will scream positive affirmations and gently coax you out of your shell and into contact with the many opportunities which abound in your world every moment of every day.

Shed the fears which overshadow your world. Create success and abundance as the only true alternatives to failure. Know beyond question that you can and you will succeed—there is no room for doubt. See it, feel it, taste it, do it, and *be* it. Make your name and your wonderfully abundant life synonymous with success.

When your dreams and visions of personal abundance and prosperity are clear and beyond doubt, success is inevitable.

Communicate your dreams, visions, and feelings to others. This doesn't mean standing on the street corner with a megaphone, but speaking from the heart to those who really matter in your life—your treasured family members and friends and those with the skills and knowledge to make a significant, positive difference in your life. You may feel awkward at first, but when you develop solid confidence and learn the value of open communication you'll begin to reap the incredible rewards. First believe in your own worth and value; others will then see you as you truly are.

Keep your focus and determination and allow enthusiasm to be your guide. Permit nothing negative to impede your forward momentum. Be open to all opportunities which come your way as you continue to listen to that inner voice. Put your plans into action right now. *Be a doer—not just a talker!*

Every time you fall and pick yourself up, you grow stronger and more determined. It in turn paves the way for success and abundance in your life.

Open your mind and your heart and live your life with love, gratitude, drive, compassion, commitment, focus, and purpose. Know that you have at your fingertips the incredible talent to build your own destiny. In this profound belief there is so much more in store for you.

Learn to trust, respect, and believe in yourself and your ability; use your heart and mind wisely. The world will become a new and exciting place to dwell.

Never say never—it becomes the longest and most immense void in your life.

Success will rarely be handed to you on a silver platter and certainly won't be found in a magic spell or potion. However, when you understand the steps necessary to bring wealth and abundance into your life, you'll not look at your world in the same way. Perhaps for the first time ever, you will hold in your hand the key to a whole new and incredibly uplifting existence.

Begin the quest today. It will open doors to limitless opportunities, lead you to countless incredible places, and give you breathtaking views of the magnificent future which awaits you. It will not always be easy, but it promises to be exciting. Open your eyes today and believe.

Drop by the website (www.kieranrevell.com) and let me know of your great successes. They will act as catalysts for so many other people seeking assistance, support and encouragement.

Join the blogs and forums and share your ideas and passions with other like-minded, driven, and successful people on their own incredible journeys. Your story might just be the motivation someone needs to assist them to step out of the shadows.

The best and most effective information is that which is freely shared and gratefully received, because *success is not a privilege!*

> Once you have a dream and a clear vision of your future, the world around you suddenly explodes with the most beautiful and vivid colors.

Have a look at my YouTube videos designed to assist and support your journey to a brand new and exciting future. I also have regular posts on various E-zine sites. The information is all designed to assist, support and encourage you to achieve all you're capable of. Suddenly, the future becomes unlimited.

I wish you every success on your incredible journey. You truly are a magnificent person, worthy of every imaginable wonder in your world. Believe that principle to be the absolute truth and all things will become possible in your glorious life.

A DICTIONARY OF EMPOWERING WORDS FOR EVERYDAY USE

Abundance: success in incredible amounts. A great quantity of everything which makes up our prosperity, whether good health and happiness, money, material wealth, or the many other aspects of success.

Acceptance: your ability to embrace a person or situation, often in spite of the ramifications. It speaks volume about you as much as the other person or circumstance.

Accountability: taking responsibility for your words and actions and their impact on others. Step up and accept liability; have the courage and fortitude to answer ethically for your life choices.

Acclaim: praise and compliments for things well done. You can never accept compliments from others until you can easily accept them from yourself.

Admiration: the high regard you have for another and that person has for you, in terms of the good you do and the respect you hold for yourself and others.

Amazing: incredible, startling, wonderful, and marvelous. When something takes your breath away and makes you feel fantastic.

Appreciation: the admiration, pleasure, and approval you have for the positive things which touch your life and the reasons why things occur as they do.

Brilliant: when a person or situation is dazzling, just spectacular, simply shining and sparkling.

Charity: giving aid and assistance to other people. It is a giving from the heart without expectation and with a genuine respect Should Read: for the welfare of others and their feelings.

Clarity: the precision and clear insight of a situation. What you bring to your life and a given situation with focus, drive, and determination. When you remove the peripheral information and leave the clear and unimpeded vision of your incredible life and journey.

Color: the light, lift, and freshness in your world or any given situation. That breath of fresh air breathed into your journey to add a whole new dimension to your life.

Commitment: your pledge to succeed. The promise or vow you make to do your best to achieve your goals.

Compassion: sympathy, kindness, and consideration toward others. Having a true concern for the welfare of others and an empathy with their position.

Congruence: when everything in our lives comes together in unprecedented accord, with all pieces fitting snugly together to give greater unity, clarity, and color to our individual journeys.

Contentment: those feelings you have of satisfaction, happiness, pleasure, and gratification when you know you are on the right track to greater prosperity. It is the warm and endearing feelings you have about yourself.

Courage: the nerve and steel to act on our convictions in the face of the overwhelming odds which we oftenencounter on our forward journey. Standing up in the face of adversity and doing what we know to be right.

Destiny: your fate or providence. A destination you desire to reach, which brings with it abundance and prosperity.

Determination: your willpower and tenacity in a situation. Your resolve to stay the distance through an unerring belief in yourself and your life in spite of the obstacles and negative circumstances you may face.

Dreams: those aspects of your life which drive you forward. The foundation upon which you build your incredible future; from which comes the color, clarity, and passion to continue on that incredible journey.

Drive: compels you forward to achieve your goals. That inner force which pushes you on even during those stressful times when you feel as if you want to quit.

Ecstasy: far stronger and more powerful than any drug. Those feelings of love, bliss, rapture, and pure excitement when you realize your world is a wonderful place to be and you can enjoy every moment of your wonderful and empowered existence.

Empowerment: the inner strength we discover when we have victory over adversity in our lives.

Enchantment: a time of fascination, charm, and delight when we feel balance and harmony in our lives.

Encouragement: the selfless support you give others in the pursuit of their goals. The enthusiasm you show for their drive to be the best they can in their lives.

Enlightenment: the period of clarification and illumination in our lives when we finally see the power we have over our existence and feel comfort with the strong and unerring belief we hold in ourselves and our individual journeys.

Enthusiasm: your keenness, fervor, and passion for a particular situation. That inner spark which drives you forward toward your goals and dreams.

Esteem: the respect, regard, and admiration in which you hold others, they hold you, and you hold for yourself.

Ethics: a program of personal moral principles by which we live our lives. Those just and decent rules of conduct which govern our lives and the way we interact with others.

Exhilaration: those feelings of happiness, excitement, and joy when you can see and feel the sunlight of opportunity and success shining in your life and you have warmth and love flood over you.

Fabulous: where a situation is tremendous; incredible, magnificent and extraordinary. Things are simply perfect and you are in harmony with the world around you. Everything is marvelous.

Focus: your inner spotlight you shine on the road, task, journey, or action ahead. The concentration on any situation to assist in reaching a satisfactory conclusion.

Faith: the ability to believe firmly in what we're doing and the path we're traveling in spite of what others might say or the problems we may encounter along the way. The inner assurance we are doing the right thing for ourselves and our families.

Fantastic: where a situation is almost beyond belief. It's truly incredible and above all expectations.

Generosity: a kindness without expectation. Giving freely from the heart, especially to those less fortunate.

Goals: principally your ambition, aims, or targets. It's the light at the end of the rainbow for which we all constantly strive.

Goodwill: the benevolence you have toward others. The kindness you show without expectation. The care and support you show toward all manner of people, regardless of their relationship to you.

Gratitude: a heartfelt thanks for things received. A true appreciation and gratefulness for a positive and warming situation.

Happiness: the feelings of elation we have when we find our life is taking us in the right direction, when we overcome obstacles and achieve our goals. It has the capacity to bring a smile to our faces.

Harmony: the accord and synchronization we have in our lives when everything is in total balance.

Honesty: a sincerity and truthfulness which should never impact negatively on others. A frankness and openness which has the ability to heal wounds, build friendships, and assist others to grow and flourish in spite of challenges faced.

Hope: the eternal optimism we hold deep inside for a better world and greater personal existence in spite of the challenges and obstacles we face. The driving force which springs forth and empowers us to continue on our journeys in spite of the hurdles we encounter.

Incredible: something unbelievable. A person or situation which is spectacular—almost beyond belief: Someone or something which fills you with absolute joy and happiness.

Insight: those inner feelings of "knowing" we have in relation to a specific topic or matter which gives us the edge.

Joy: feelings of elation when we're touched by something wonderful in our lives bringing flooding feelings of warmth.

Knowledge: that awareness and understanding of what we're doing; the true insight into the power of our goals and a unique perception of the value of the life we're leading.

Longevity: your durability and endurance. That ability to maintain the level of empowerment, drive, and commitment in your journey.

Love: the wonderful, warm, and all-encompassing feeling of contentment and acceptance we find in a non-judgmental relationship with ourselves and others, in spite of our flaws and shortcomings.

Magnificence: the brilliance and radiance which shines from a particular person or situation. That specific aspect which makes the difference between ordinary and extraordinary.

Morals: the principles of conduct governing our everyday lives. There is a vast distinction between what is right and proper and what is incorrect, wrong, and inappropriate, especially in our dealings with others.

Openness: an honesty and sincerity which will attract others to you; laying yourself open to scrutiny and giving freely of yourself—your skills, respect, love, and experience.

Optimism: the joy, openness, and buoyancy you have, generally in times of stress or overwhelming pressure when you can retain your vision and focus in spite of what is thrown at you.

Optimum: the best possible and most favorable level in regard to achievement. The best of the best.

Passion: an excitement and enthusiasm for what we do. An inner driving force which gives us the power and determination to achieve our goals.

Patience: tolerance, persistence, and fortitude in spite of the trials and tribulations faced daily. Your ability to stay the distance and find plausible solutions to the problems you face. Nothing is insurmountable.

Peace of mind: the calmness and serenity which envelops us when our lives are on track and we know beyond question we're traveling in the right direction.

Perception: your insight into and awareness of a particular situation. Your "knowing" and alertness to those things which can impact you.

Perseverance: your resolve and determination to go the distance in spite of the challenges you may face along the way.

Persistence: the tenacity and doggedness you can muster in the face of overwhelming odds. The commitment to the challenge and sheer determination to achieve your goals.

Phenomenal: where something is extraordinary, exceptional, and unique. It can apply to a situation, opportunity, thought, or action.

Pride: those overall feelings of tremendous satisfaction, pleasure, and delight we have when we at last realize the enormity of our achievements, the strides we've taken, and the path our incredible life is now traveling.

Prosperity: Wealth, riches, richness, and affluence. A birthright of us all, irrespective of current circumstances.

Purpose: a reason or intention. Your purpose in this life is to do the best you can with the skills you have and the determination you hold to be incredibly successful in spite of what life might throw at you.

Recognition: that aspect of success which brings you accolades and attention for your good work, success, and/or generosity. The positive way others perceive you and respond accordingly.

Remarkable: when a situation is just outstanding. Where what you do and see is just so special and astonishing.

Respect: the admiration and esteem in which you are held by others and that same deference you have toward them.

Responsibility: taking ownership of your words and actions and their impact on others. Being accountable for what you do in life; ensuring your behavior is moral and above reproach.

Sanguine: confident, optimistic, cheerful, positive, and upbeat. How we should all try to feel every day to empower and inspire ourselves to even greater achievements.

Self-esteem: Your degree of confidence in yourself as others see you and your ability to rise above adversity, to accept challenges, and to acknowledge triumph over adversity.

Self-respect: your decision to respect yourself and be the best you can in spite of life's challenges. Others will never respect you if you don't respect yourself.

Self-worth: the sense of worth you hold for yourself, reflected in the amount of love and admiration you have for who you are, the life you lead, and the way you positively interact with others.

Success: An achievement, accomplishment, or triumph. That superb objective for which we continue to strive. An intricate component of our goals; an integral part of the light at the end of the tunnel.

Terrific: a situation which is wonderful. Everything about it is excellent—quite remarkable.

Thankfulness: the showing of gratitude and appreciation for all that's great in one's existence. Being heartily thankful for everything which adds color, depth, passion, and meaning to life.

Togetherness: that feeling of warmth and acceptance in a union—whether immediate family, neighbors, community, or global. It means being in a union with like-minded people where there is acceptance and a focus on a common vision. Everyone and all things in harmony.

Tolerance: your acceptance of a person or situation. Your ability to remain level headed and enduring, in spite of any differences or misgivings you may have.

Tremendous: fantastic, remarkable, incredible, terrific. The way we should describe our lives every day.

Triumphant: proud, victorious, successful. How we feel when we've done something truly exceptional.

Trust: a firm belief in the honesty and respect of others which comes from an understanding of our own worth. The total ability to move forward on our own judgment and courage to act on that intense feeling of "right."

Truth: a fact, reality, or certainty in a situation. It means to be open and honest in dealings with others. It brings its own rewards.

Understanding: being considerate, thoughtful, and accepting of others. Having a kindness for their feelings. Being perceptive of the needs of others.

Verve: the vitality, energy, and spirit you put into your life, which adds energy and passion to your every moment.

Wealth: the affluence, prosperity, and abundance found in an empowered and enriched existence.

Wisdom: the accumulated mental power which comes from living life. A real unique and in-depth understanding of what it means to truly comprehend the world around us.

Wonder: The magic and splendor of a given situation. That special something which makes our spirits sour and hearts sing.

Zest: Your keenness, passion and enthusiasm for your life and everything it brings.

The difference between successful people and those who are forever chasing that elusive prize is the determination, passion, drive, and commitment they display in and for their lives and their destinies.

Whatever you do in and with your life, your actions should be well-intentioned and receive the drive, commitment, and respect they deserve. Give real and heartfelt credit to everything you achieve, each empowering thought you have, and every encouraging word you utter. Treat every aspect of your life with absolute respect.

Develop an unfathomable love for yourself and your life and be grateful for every wonderful component of your glorious existence. The more genuine gratitude you have, the more wonderful things will begin to manifest in your life.

Have pride in the person you are and the individual you strive to be. Continue to live in harmony with your core values and beliefs. Never compromise your dignity or respect, and fill every moment with love, gratitude, and dedication to the cause of building the best and most prosperous life possible.

> Never underestimate the value of self-worth. It is one of the most wonderful and empowering assets you possess.

There is a genius, millionaire, successful entrepreneur, award-winning author, actor, designer, champion athlete, race car driver, deep sea diver, jet pilot, engineer, scientist, tennis professional, or mountaineer residing within each of us. We need only recognize the person we strive to be and make up our minds to embrace the success we desire in a timely fashion, driven by our plan of action and fired by a fierce and unrestrained determination to reach our goals. The horizon might not always be in sight, but know with certainty it is there and is reachable.

The wonderfully inspiring Art E. Berg was a missionary, sports champion, author, and motivational speaker; he was also a quadriplegic. He lived his incredible life by the adage, "While the difficult takes time, the impossible just takes a little longer!"[1] Believe all things are possible. Know that life can be a challenge. Understand that on some days, your future might seem out of reach. Be confident your life will be filled with smiles, laughter, tears, anger, frustration, faith, love, tolerance, commitment, impatience, happiness, loss, excitement, praise, criticism, generosity, respect, truth, courage, elation, acceptance, drive, compassion, gratitude, confidence, trust, self-respect, understanding, doubt, exhilaration, and triumph.

Know undeniably that success and abundance are your birth rights and with drive, passion, and determination you can achieve all you desire.

> All things in life are truly within your grasp, no matter how unachievable they can at first appear. Believe beyond question that you can realize enormous prosperity and are totally deserving of true success. The journey has already begun.

Create your own perfect life—the ideal existence. A world in which there is rich color, warmth, love, and power. A place where you are fit and healthy, happy and inspired. It exists right now, but it's your task to find it and uncover the wealth of opportunities to mold it as you wish.

Find the horizon—that clear and unambiguous point of victory and achievement ahead on your roadmap to success. It will continually change as you reach one milestone and constantly and confidently stride for another. That's the power and wonder of opportunity.

When you fall down, confront an obstacle, or wander from the path, it won't always be easy to get back on track and continue with the same passion and purpose. However, it is possible if you find inside the deep-seated commitment to success. Remind yourself why you are making the effort and keep the images of the ideal life at the forefront of your mind.

Never stop believing in yourself, your life, and your incredible creativity. You have a wonderful life. You'll begin to live it to the full as you realize that the possibilities for an extraordinary future are truly endless. You need only open your mind and remain passionate and positive. Your life will change in exceptional ways.

NOTES

1. Art E. Berg, https://www.goodreads.com/author/quotes/200140.Art_E_Berg.

> The magic of success lies not simply in what you say
> but in what you do and the determination, focus, and
> self-belief you employ in that empowering task.

LESSONS LEARNED

The power of the human spirit is virtually unfathomable. We have a depth and diversity which will never be crushed or curtailed as long as we hold on to our dreams and visions of a better and more inspired life and do everything positive and enriching within our power to see them materialize.

Use at least a dozen of the above words every day of your life to enhance all aspects of your existence. In this way you are continuing to build a solid and structured framework for a new and all-encompassing existence.

Rather than being your own worst enemy through negativity, hesitation, and procrastination, you will slowly but surely become the greatest asset you possess. Treasure your life; love yourself always.

As you begin to value the wonderful things you have in your life now, you'll understand the power of appreciation for your eventual prosperity.

ABOUT KIERAN REVELL

After every storm which enters my life sunshine soon follows, provided I welcome it and have laid the foundation for success and harmony.

From his childhood and through his teenage years, Kieran Revell suffered under the weight of an almost unbearable speech stammer. Coupled with a near-drowning experience at age 17, where he is convinced he received messages from his long passed grandparents (part of which was for him to 'tap into the unstoppable power within himself'), the early life challenges has seen him embark on a life long journey of discovery and fulfillment. He has made it his mission to assist others—corporate leaders, business owners and individuals to add depth, color and diversity to their lives. It has become an extraordinary journey of personal and professional realization.

He has since gone on to become an international executive leadership consultant and speaker, mentor and author. He specializes in Spiritual Leadership Wisdom.

He has studied the many aspects of personal development for over 25 years. Inspiration, determination, focus, and gratitude remain constants in his approach to fulfilment.

With the right attitude and a passion for life, you can achieve anything.

Kieran's knowledge, passion, and advanced programs deliver the tools, resources, and strategies necessary for individuals and corporations to step out of the shadows and grow.

He assists clients to improve workplace harmony, nurture and encourage team spirit, strengthen personal and professional relationships, reignite self-confidence and respect, develop effective communication skills, streamline goals, and maximize human potential and peak performance in the realization of unimaginable dreams.

A sought-after keynote speaker, Kieran believes totally in the power of "the self," and through his warm and optimistic nature he empowers individuals, groups, and corporations to understand and appreciate the inherent ability to achieve extraordinary growth.

Every day I do the best I can with the tools I have. I know it is bringing success and abundance into my life.

Kieran's functional programs clear pathways to greater success and empowerment. They enable clients to discover a wider appreciation of life through initiating improvement strategies for the instigation of a functional work/life balance and stronger and longer lasting personal and professional relationships.

Kieran teaches effective culture change initiatives in unique and upbeat corporate, group, and individual training programs. A fresh and driven thought leader, he uncovers the gifts of determination, focus, communication, and action in clients enabling them to connect the dots joining dreams to reality—the skills and knowledge necessary to transform lives.

Kieran's strategies constantly challenge individuals and corporations to clear obstacles in their processes to expedite the realization of brilliant performance. This enables the achievement of even greater levels of engagement, retention, and productivity, leading to a remarkable bottom line.

Success fills my life because self-belief is a fundamental component of my existence.

Effective communication is a vitally important component for growth and development in both your personal and professional spheres. Kieran is a specialist who inspires comprehensive and dynamic interaction. His disarming nature and passion for life help to break down barriers, unlock the power within, and rebuild strong and functional channels. Unleash your power today.

Kieran has always been fascinated by the science of success and all it embodies. Why do some people succeed where others do not, and why does a percentage of the population appear to corner the market on wealth and abundance when others struggle their whole lives with little to show for their efforts? These and many other questions continue to fire his passion and imagination. His strategies and programs help to deliver the answers.

> If you are unable to hold success in your heart, you'll never hold it in your hands.

This book outlines the systematic action Kieran believes is necessary to build an exceptional existence and achieve an extraordinary quality of life, as he has done.

Kieran is available for your next seminar, event, or coaching session when you make up your mind to put yourself, your family, and your business/company/group on the pathway to indescribable success and prosperity. Take positive action today to transform your dreams into reality.

Turn the key of opportunity in your life right now and unlock your magnificent future. Have faith in all you know you are capable of becoming. Don't procrastinate, because the greatest obstacle to success is your own failure to believe.

> I'm traveling the exhilarating and exciting road to incredible abundance because I'm persistent, focused, committed, and happy.

Imagine the possibilities.

FURTHER PUBLICATIONS

This book is the first in a series by the author. Each is designed to enrich and empower the reader.

The information is of immeasurable value to corporate leaders, business owners, and individuals seeking that edge to further develop their business and professional lives so as to enrich and empower the great global community.

In the next book, the author continues the amazing journey of personal and professional development.

Imagine the possibilities.